LEADERSHIP HABITS

**INSPIRING STORIES AND STRATEGIES THAT
WILL HELP YOU LEAD WITH SUCCESS.**

FELIPE AGREDANO • HUGO BALTA • DAMIANO RAIGOZA • REY III VIQUEZ
MARCOS OROZCO • JOEL LOPEZ GARCIA • ROLANDO CASTRO

Disclaimer: Thank you for buying and reading this book. The authors wanted to share their experience and knowledge with you that could potentially improve the quality of your life and the lives of others. Spanish is the native tongue for all of the authors and this is their first of many books. Despite their noble intentions, this book will have mistakes like any other book. If you find any mistakes, **PLEASE** tell us by sending the error and page you found it on to our email **LeadershipHabitsBook@gmail.com.** We thank you and appreciate your feedback. We would like to wish only the best for you and your families.

CONNECT WITH THE AUTHORS!!

Please register by visiting the website, and get instant access to **videos** that connects you to each author. Simply go to:

www.LeadershipHabitsBook.com

CONTENTS

INTRODUCTION

Leadership Habits is a book that was written out of necessity. Our country is soon going to elect a new president and we have never been more divided than ever before. Most people think that the decisions of the new President will improve or diminish their quality of life but in all reality this is normally not the case. The upcoming market correction will most definitely make a greater impact on the life of your family and loved ones and it does not discriminate against political affiliation, race, gender or common beliefs. This book was written by 7 Latino authors who united together and are dedicated to improving the quality of life of our people and communities. It's time for American Latinos to unite together along with other ethnicities to take a stand for a better tomorrow for our children. The world is hungry for leadership and we want to contribute our experiences in this book.

CHAPTER ONE

FELIPE AGREDANO-LOZANO

One of the greatest misconceptions about leadership is that it is about one individual. The common belief is one person leads many people to success or victory. However, Paul's Epistle to the Galatians teaches us to be servants to one another and nowhere is that more true than in the quest to be leaders. Whether Christian, Jewish, Muslim, or even non-believer, we can agree that leadership requires a commitment to community. Like everything, it begins with being beholden to one another. One of my mentors and former professors, Dr. Cornel West teaches, "You can't lead the people if you don't love the people.

You can't save the people if you don't serve the people." If we are to truly love one another as my bible tells me so, we must develop relationships without judgement or a quest for authority but develop them out of a true love for our community.

I learned these lessons at an early age. I grew up in a Latino Apostolic Pentecostal home. My parents immigrated to the Los Angeles in 1968 from a little town named Las Cruces, Cuquío in Los Altos, near Guadalajara, Jalisco. While many people were attending the Olympics in Mexico City my parents were headed north. I was born in the Boyle Heights community of the City of Los Angeles, near 4th and Soto Streets. My parents lived in East Los Angeles on Rowan Street but my family later moved to South Central Los Angeles. There was a community shift occurring in this area of Southeast Los Angeles County. At that time White fi ght was taking place in Huntington Park and the population was quickly shifting to a solid Latino immigrant majority. Latinos were moving to the area, my family among them, because they saw doors opening there that were not opening in other parts of the city. They were able to grow businesses, purchase houses and create a life among people that welcomed them. This newly created Southeast LA identity developed into a dynamic hotbed of immigrant life and activity.

Being a part of that renaissance along with the strong emphasis my parents placed on hard work and a solid education helped me to see at an early age that we are all connected. We all have a responsibility toward each other to serve in a way that adds to the common good. My father worked very hard and was fi nally able to purchase a "carniceria," a small butcher shop. He taught me the trade of daily meat preparation such as storing, sorting, chopping, pricing, and selling "carne fresca" to our immigrant clientele. Working at the family

business strongly impacted my way of life. I saw daily the passion and dedication with which my parents ran their business. The fi rst year I helped my father stock the store. I quickly learned how to be a merchant and retailer. Because of the family's focus providing service to the local Latino clients, I became very dedicated to the community. But my parents wanted more for me.

As important as hard work was to my family, they also wanted me to get a solid education. My father was orphaned before he was 10 years old. He did not have the opportunity to fi nish school, much less an opportunity to attend college in Mexico. My mom attended high school, but my grandfather did not allow her to go on to university. In those days he only allowed the men in the family to continue their education. Of my mother's three brothers, one became a medical doctor, one an attorney, and another an engineer. Education was defi nitely highly-valued and integral part of their background, even if it was just for the males. Although my mother did not attend college, she was very active in the community, politics, and her local union.

When it came to their children it was of great importance that they all earn college degrees. I didn't really know how I would accomplish that, but I knew I had to fi gure it out. I had no clue which college or university I would attend, but I defi nitely knew that I would be going to college. I began the transition from high school to college lacking guidance and direction. My earliest memories of grammar school are at State Street School, Middleton Street School, then Henry T. Gage Jr. High in Huntington Park and eventually a few classes at Huntington Park High School. Half of my schooling was in within the Los Angeles Unifi ed School District, (LAUSD) but I graduated from the Accelerated Christian Education (ACE School), a fundamentalist-leaning educational schooling center in Latino urban Huntington

Park, Southeast Los Angeles County. Challenges both academic and personal expectations were constantly going through my head. I could not decide where to attend and what to study when I got there. I started at my local public community college, East Los Angeles College

(ELAC). Once there as a full-time student, I learned I could transfer and discovered what financial aid and scholarships were. ELAC was a first step for many Latino students trying to figure out not only how to access higher education but also who they were going to become. It also provided opportunities for students to be politically involved for the first time in their lives. I was no different. I not only found educational direction at ELAC, I found an activism that has stayed with me ever since my days there.

"Yo no estudio para saber mas, sino para ignorar menos"

- Sor Juana Inez de la Cruz

I applied to UC Berkeley, UCLA, and UC San Diego and was accepted at all three public institutions. UC Berkeley captivated me and I spent some of my most memorable years there. I received my education and earned my Bachelor's degree there and opened the door to further my education. I applied to Harvard University, was accepted and completed my Master's program. I am proud to add that both my siblings received a college education. Starting with my sister Denise Ninette at the community college level and my younger brother Obed continued on to UCLA, Columbia and finishing in a Doctoral program.

At Harvard, I worked with many of the students from around the world. In particular, I met many Latina/os coming from other prestigious Ivy League schools. We were well organized and active at the Divinity School with activist students. I was involved with the Harvard Divinity School Council and The Harvard Graduate Student

Council. We created the first Harvard University Latino student council named Concilio Latino de Harvard with Latina/o students. It encompassed all the campus-wide organizations which included over a dozen undergraduate and eleven graduate student and organizations:

such as Luz Herrera and Raquel Aldana at Harvard Law School; David
Cazares at Harvard Business School; Adolfo Mendez and Chris Tirres
at Harvard Divinity School; Cindy Sanchez, Jose Moreno, Haydee Diaz,
Paul Correa, Danielle Carrigo, and Luis Ayala at the Harvard Graduate
School of Education; and, Irma Muñoz, Russ Calleros, and Leo Carrillo
at the Kennedy School of Government. I learned much of working
together in collaboration from my years at UC Berkeley. My personal
and professional mentors at CAL were Prof. Larry Trujillo, Dr. Lupe
Gallegos-Diaz and my academic mentor was Dr. Margarita Melville. At
Harvard University I was mentored by Dr. Cornel West, Dr. Harvey Cox
and my personal friend June Erlick.

Higher Educational institutions such as UC Berkeley and Harvard
helped open the door for me to come out and work with my Latino
and LGBT communities. Peer mentor role-models in undergraduate
and graduate students like Veronica Terriquez, Alfred Fraijo, Ana-
Maurine Lara, Eddie González-Novoa, and Raul Gómez assisted me
in this process. There I also helped organize Harvard's fi rst Latino
graduation, and the fi rst Latino Welcome Day collectively with
other students. In 2016, Harvard celebrated the 20th Anniversary
of the Harvard Public Policy, Law and Business Conference, where
fellow Latina/o alumni and I served as key leaders in organizing and
spearheading these collaborative projects between Irma Munoz, Leo
Carrillo and Luz Herrera. What I learned there was how to connect
people, listen and work toward a common good for all and negotiating
and creating eff ective win-win solutions.

As a kid, I played in the dirt, building roads, homes and bridges –
I created things with my hands, and I would also demolish them
by blowing them up with fi recrackers to again build up. Looking
back, perhaps I should have become a city planner, an architect or

draftsman. I believe I'm a social engineer, because I enjoy building things together. I miss playing in the dirt, building bridges, building roads and connecting places to each other. Connecting people to places with real functional bridges made of dirt was my youth. Today, I'm still connecting bridges, but now with community, reinvestment and advocacy, (CRA). I still do this but at a more human level. The bridges I connect, are no longer made of dirt bridges, they are now people and projects. I am a social engineer, I have become the bridge.

Education was a priority to both parents. One particular time I remember, my 14th birthday, when I received a very heavy box, as a gift from my father. I imagined it to be something really cool. I saved it to be the last present I opened. To my surprise, this box turned out to be carrying a huge Webster's encyclopedic dictionary and it was quite heavy to pick up. I remember at the time I realized what it was. I wasn't excited about an encyclopedic dictionary. My gift would also become my educational torture device and it was my internet. But I learned everything I needed to know was in that heavy book. Heavy with information, it served to educate and give me a firm learning foundation. My father knew exactly what he was doing.

Later in life I figured this out. He had managed to instill in me the value of education, education and more education, interspersed with lots of hard work. Together we worked hard as a family, helping the family business grow. I learned everything apprenticeship style in that carniceria. The family expectation always was that I'd be going to college. During grammar school years at State Street and Middleton of

LAUSD schools and in high school at my local parish, ACE school, there was a continued emphasis on studying and graduating from college. I attended High School during the day and took college courses at night at East LA College. Every weekend and holiday I'd work in "La carniceria", with little or no time to play. Any time I was not in school, I was going to college or working.

LEADERSHIP

> "A genuine leader is not a searcher for consensus
> but a molder of consensus."
>
> - Martin Luther King, Jr.

I grew up in an Apostolic Christian home and was exposed to both community and faith-based leadership I began to develop my leadership skills at a very young age that continued into East LA College and through Harvard. I credit my local church involvement as a place of dynamic, highly-immigrant, social justice and higher education supporting church. Instrumental in this were my visionary pastors Rev. Hilario Gámez and Sister Ester Muro with immigrant roots from Nayarit and Sinaloa, Mexico. Huntington Park Apostolic Church was perhaps one of, if not the most forward thinking churches within the Apostolic Assembly denomination, with a congregation of well over 1,500 attendees and over 5,000 individuals within its sphere of infl uence. Upwards of 30 churches trace early leadership roots to this congregation with its highly eff ective organic grassroots leadership. One important leadership quality, I developed was to be an active listener. I developed and honed these skills in all organizations I was involved with. I strive to always listen to constituents', the organizations goals and the project set out to accomplish.

Another characteristic of good leadership is the ability to connect. I connect with people, connect to a project in order to execute a plan. It is essential for me to look at avenues of opportunities, connect strengths, values and identify weaknesses too. Together we determine how to adjust, prepare and anticipate areas to be strengthened. A brain child and accomplishment I am most proud of is HONOR PAC, a Latina/o LGBT political action committee that originated in Los Angeles, spread statewide and has grown to national prominence in supporting and electing close to 100 Latina/o LGBT o ffi ce holders in various states. We connected on the mission to elect openly progressive LGBT Latina/os and allies.

An important trait of leadership is also the ability to execute. You can listen to a committee, listen to diff erent varied ideas, diff erent stakeholders, simultaneously connect, but you must always be sure when and how to execute. I am too familiar with the term of 'death by committee.' Too often, great ideas and projects get lost, shuffl ed and die in committee. A good leader will navigate through this and a diversity of voices to execute a project or a plan and carry it through to survival. I am also proud to have been off ered an opportunity to serve as a national Board Member for the Asociacion Lideres Hispanos whose mission is to support relationship between the United States and Spain. Serving has allowed me to listen, connect and execute several international business and trade missions to Spain and Mexico via Washington D.C.

FAITH, HOPE AND CHARITY

Remember you live in a community. You have a responsibility to be accountable to your family and your community as well as yourself.

– Cherrie Moraga

It is vital to give back to our community. Everything I have built, was through hard work and education. However, my family immigrant experience, community, and this great nation have all helped me develop into the person I am today. It's a value instilled in me early through my family, church and community. I was given great opportunities therefore it's important to give back to society.

I am very proud of building communities. By doing so, I was able to execute Bank of America's largest event in the nation, right here in Los Angeles, California. BofA had attempted a large scale event in Texas and in New York. However, it was in Los Angeles where we were able to execute the number one and best attended event for Bank of America by working and building with the community. I was also able to develop Freddie Mac's number one event in California. Additionally, I was able to execute one of National Council of La Raza's (NCLR) top two events in the nation, second only to Florida.

I am most proud of the national impact we had with NCLR in passing the California Homeowner Bill of Rights. By working directly with communities, we created the first landmark legislation in the country which served as a blueprint for other states in the nation. Working with faith leaders and J.P. Morgan Chase & Co., I lead a Latino prayer breakfast for housing and for financial literacy to effectively fight the financial and housing crisis in California and the nation. Also, with Southern California Edison and Latina/o faith leaders, we partnered on energy and utilities.

CRAstategies.org

Under the Community Reinvestment Act, (CRA) the banks must provide modest income and low-income families with loans for the purchase of homes that they can afford. What I do at CRAstrategies.

org is help banks hit their targets. I make sure funders are able to find the communities in need and are able to maximize their efforts by hitting the targets that they need.

"To whom much is given, much is expected"

– Gospel of Luke

Many of these opportunities have come through working with communities and faith-based partnerships. When, working with Southern California Edison, we had the first Latino prayer breakfast. We've executed a few other of these prayer breakfasts in Los Angeles with AltaMed, the University of Southern California, (USC), J.P. Morgan Chase & Co. and Edison. It's been a wonderful journey to be able to work with all of the community. Across different issues, such as housing, financial education, health, or working with faith-based communities and elected leaders, I've been able to bring people together to the table bringing diverse constituencies and carrying them through to execute top-notch programs and deliver some of the top events has been very rewarding.

CHALLENGES

"Not all of us can do great things.
But we can do small things with great love."

- Mother Teresa of Calcutta

Undoubtedly there have been challenges. Some of these have been not being able to help the community in tough times like the great recession. During the housing crisis and the financial instability in California and our country, there were certain occasions that we could not help families secure their homes. Many lost their homes and

became homeless. There were times we cried together with families. No matter how hard we tried to tackle issues, we were not able to help. Those were some of the darker times, where as a professional, as an individual, a person of faith, you're not able to help despite your best eff orts.

AGREDANO-LOZANO AND ASSOCIATES

I change myself, I change the world.

- Gloria Anzaldua

Today, at Agredano-Lozano and Associates, we focus on CRA solutions. You can fi nd us at CRAstrategies.org, where we connect faith-based leaders, elected o ffi cials, community organizations and corporate partners. Together we work to off er fi nancial literacy education, create the wellness for folks that need the education, and the housing opportunities needed to create wealth. We work to provide access to loans for families, fi nancial literacy and fi nancial education as well. As families develop wealth, to pass it on to the next generation, we fi nd housing advocates and connect them to communities in need of services that help them grow fi nancially.

BUILDING BRIDGES

I've had many bridges in my life and background, I personally really like the old 6th Street Bridge in Los Angeles. It connects Los Angeles' Downtown to the East Side. A new 6th Street bridge project is coming to Los Angeles and the eastside. I see bridges as a testament to my education, career and to my professional development. Perhaps, in some way, I am a bridge. I love to connect people to people. I love

to connect projects. I like to connect the community and community development with the banks and the corporations, and I love to connect faith-based leaders. I love to connect people. It's in me. It's in my DNA. Connection is part of what I do. Maybe I am a bridge after all.

Today's children instead of building bridges of dirt often have the opportunity of playing virtual reality games such as SimCity with scenarios like Flint, Michigan, which has gone through economic distress. Having an opportunity to fi x the roads, infrastructure, increase business development, attract and grow the population and develop a quality place to live.

Sim City gives the player a scenario of a community in need. Much like Huntington Park, where I grew up. When companies leave an area, they go into depression, During the White fl ight that had occurred because Firestone and Bethlehem Steel and many big companies left. There were no more jobs and went into an economic depression. However, it created opportunities for immigrants to come, reinvest and be part, and rebuild Huntington Park and the Southeast communities into a stronger community.

Huntington Park became a miracle mile and I learned this while taking a class at Harvard. On a visit to Harvard, Dr. Wayne Cornelius founder and director of the Center for Comparative Immigration Studies at UC San Diego shared this very valuable lesson. The whole mile of Pacifi c Boulevard beat out Beverly Hills and Downtown Los Angeles in fi nancial volume. Huntington Park won in an economic competition, because there were more small transactions occurring, more sales more frequently to become the economic stimulus for the Southeast of LA County. County-wide, there were more jobs, increased wealth creation, additional businesses being developed in Huntington Park

than in Downtown Los Angeles on Broadway or on Rodeo Drive in Beverly Hills.

When I learned this I thought to myself, "Wow! Here's my very modest community of Huntington Park, beating and being an impressive place that provides local opportunities for the community and also a conduit for global transactions". An international dynamic of trade, globalization, creating opportunities for immigrants and one that strengthens the economic area which had survived through economic depression and thrived! Immigration really revitalized businesses, energized and galvanized a whole corridor, bringing it back to life. It was the immigrant community who brought this city back to life.

RETROSPECT

> Our prime purpose in this life is to help others.
> And if you can't help them, at least don't hurt them.
>
> – Dalai Lama

I learned that you reach a limit of what you're able to do. From that, you learn that you need to have other strategies in how to regenerate people, individuals and families. I learned how to provide services for the next person. Families that might have lost their homes, we talked about re-housing, and resolved their situation. They were helping to tap into services where they were able to pay their bills, re-integrate into society and restore fi nancial wealth and security.

I've had several mentors, but I'll narrow it down to two. In my educational career, my mentor was my graduate school professor, Dr. Cornel West, he infl uenced me and motivated me but most of all he inspired me. Dr. West was a very dynamic leader, a person who really engaged his students to think. He connected with students an d had

the foresight to see us maximize our leadership potential. He was not afraid to be a public scholar, and show what true freedom really is.

My greatest mentor, profession-wise, was the honorable Reverend Dr. Jack Scott, State Senator of California, he was both a retired college president, a professor, a legislator and came from a ministerial background. With him, I really connected in terms of the ministry of public service and how we can better serve our community through public policy, social service, while coming from a very deep and meaningful place.

THINGS I LOVE

> "El mundo debería reírse más,
> pero después de haber comido."
>
> - Cantinfl as

One thing that I really enjoy is teaching at East Los Angeles College, where I started my college career. It is professionally rewarding for me to be teaching college in the Southeast of LA, because it's very close to my heart. It's where I grew up. It's the community that I know, and that I love. It really is a rewarding experience for me. I love to be back in my community.

On a more personal note, I love my family, I love to travel, and I enjoy food. I live to have a good coff ee with a friend: I love Thai, Italian, Chinese and Mexican cuisines. I love food.
EDITING TEAM: I would personally like to thank all the friends who helped me read and made valuable suggestions in the process of editing this chapter and book project: Abel Alvarado, Felipe Chavez Valladolid, Christine Senteno, Ulisses Sanchez, and Jeannette Soriano.

BIOGRAPHY

Felipe Agredano, is a Founder of Start-ups that bridge technology, project funding, community development and outreach. He is college professor and serves on the National Board of Asociación Líderes Hispanos, served as President of the School Board, President of the LA County Commission on Human Relations, Chair of CA Democratic Party's 49th Assembly District, and Founder of HonorPAC and is an alumnus of NALEO's CA Health Leadership Project.

Agredano earned an Associate of Arts at East LA College; dual Bachelor's from UC Berkeley in Government and Chicano Studies, a Masters from Harvard University and three Fellowships at the University of Oxford, la Universidad Menendez Pelayo, Santander Spain and in Italy.

A Harvard O ffi cer who served at the David Rockefeller Center for Latin American Studies, Research Assistant at the W.E.B. Du Boise Institute, Teaching Fellow for Afro-American Studies and as administrator at Radcliff e College. He served as Senior Field Representative for the Chair of the Higher Education in the State Senate. He teaches academic courses in: Politics; History of World Religions; US Political and Social History; and Religion and Chicanos at East Los Angeles College, Los Angeles Trade Tech College, Cal State, Northridge and Harvard University.

Felipe provided editing and research experience on such notable publications as The Dictionary of Global Cultures published by Kwame Anthony Appiah and Henry Louis Gates, Jr. He published several times in Harvard's Journal for Latin American Studies ReVista and was guest researcher for the "Study for Behavioral Health Studies", in the American Journal of Public Health" 2003. A frequently invited guest at local and national UNIVISION programs like "Aqui y Ahora", Felipe has appeared on CNN, NBC/Telemundo, FOX, TV Estrella, and has been quoted in The Los Angeles Times, La Opinion, and The Harvard Crimson.

Making an impact on every environment inhabited, his accolades include the distinction as "Democrat of the Year", "Young Hispanic American Leader", by the Government of Spain and "Future Leader" by La Opinion, the nation's largest Spanish-language daily.

Felipe Agredano-Lozano is the Startup Founder and CEO of Agredano-Lozano and Associates which bridges technology, project funding, community development and outreach. He earned a Bachelor of Arts degree from the University of California at Berkeley and Master's Degree from Harvard University. He was born and still resides in Los Angeles.

CHAPTER TWO
HUGO BALTA

HELLO, MI NOMBRE ES HUGO BALTA

That's OO-go, not HYOO-go. I knew I was different on the first day of kindergarten when the teacher called out the student's names to check classroom attendance.

"HYOO-go?" "HYOO-go", she asked. It wasn't until she added my last name that I realized she was referring to me. "HYOO-go Balta", she asked.

I turned to her and said, "OO-go. My name is OO-go".

"No", she said. "In English it's HYOO-go". Children are taught to respect authority and there is no higher power for a child on their first day of school than the teacher. So, I conformed or as conservatives and the like often say - I assimilated. My name was OO-go at home and HYOO-go as soon as I stepped outside.

When I returned home that day and confronted my mother with the day's event she simply and almost unsympathetically said to me, "En la casa hablas español y afuera ingles."

It took a little bit of time to digest the explanation of how things just are, but that one commandment given to me by my mother at the age of 5 had such a profound Big Bang type of effect on me that it is still shaping who I am today.

All children ever want is to be like everyone else; be accepted by their peers. It quickly became real to me that full acceptance would never be achieved.

Just how different I was became even more apparent to me when I visited Peru, my parents' native country each summer vacation. There I was known as "El Gringuito", a foreigner from Los Estados Unidos. It didn't matter that both my parents were Peruvian, my birth certificate read U.S.A.

It wasn't any better when I returned home to New Jersey. There I was a foreigner too. My name was different, my skin tone was a little darker, I spoke a different language and my parents had a funny accent. It was clear to the kids in my neighborhood that I wasn't from around here.

Not Peruvian enough.

Not American enough.

This dilemma was a defining moment in my young life. I could've rebelled and rejected all things Peruvian beginning with Spanish, but my mother intervened.

She said, "hijito, esta bien que eres diferente. Ser diferente es ser especial." She empowered me and showed me the gifts of being a child of two worlds.

It's a quality which has greatly enriched my personal and professional life. I am an experienced and award winning Broadcast and Digital Media professional directing growth, change and innovation in several divisions and businesses for English and Spanish language media in the U.S. and Latin America.

My career includes working within established structures, but applying entrepreneurial strategies in establishing new processes and working with new technology in developing and producing content.

As Senior Director of Multicultural Content at ESPN Digital and Print Media, I implement intersectional thinking in nurturing relationships to generate messages relevant to multicultural audiences across all platforms; often launching new programming.

I work with different businesses such as Sales and Publicity in identifying opportunities to engage audiences with dynamic brands.

TOGETHER WE WIN OR LOSE.

My story begins in the cradle of the industrial revolution, Paterson, New Jersey where I was born. The city's part in the American Revolution was in utilizing the energy from the Great Falls of the Passaic River. It enabled economic independence from British manufacturers. Among the industries which sprung up from harnessing such power were textile, silk, firearms and railroad locomotives. These employment opportunities were a draw for immigrant laborers including my parents.

Hugo Balta Sr. was 22 years-old when he arrived in Paterson in the early 1960's. Graciela Zavala was only 18 when she set foot in the same city a few years later. In an age when most young people are celebrating finishing high school and beginning the next chapter of their higher education, Hugo and Graciela were desperate. They were thousands of miles away from home in a foreign land where they didn't know the language or culture.

I'm 46 years old, educated and experienced. I would be more frightened than I care to admit if you were to tell me that tomorrow I had to pack up my belongings and do the same thing. Thanks to my parents I will never have to know what that type of desperation feels like. However, I do know the type of courage it takes because I was witness to it.

My father worked two jobs; one was at an automotive assembly line. Both forced him to leave our home in early morning before sunrise and come back in the evening after sunset. I have many memories of my father during my childhood, but nothing as vivid as him sleeping. The times I saw him in our apartment were mostly of him resting from a very long day's work.

It wasn't any easier for my mother. She too had multiple jobs including taking care of me. I tagged along many times as she cleaned offices and houses. She also worked in sweatshops sewing clothes. In the summer I would go visit her during lunch breaks seeing her drenched in sweat from the unbearable heat.

My father never finished high school. My mother couldn't afford a college education. But, together we switched the tassel on my graduation cap; my diploma had many recipients.

I've been fortunate to have had many more accomplishments since then. I've also had my share of setbacks. Through it all my parents and my family have directly or indirectly been involved. They selflessly lift me on their shoulders and help me reach higher and see farther than I ever will on my own two feet.

Leaders support the people around them. Part of my responsibility as a manager is to create a workplace environment where colleagues collaborate across functions and departments in order to achieve singular and collective goals. No one person can claim victory or defeat. It's been my experience that success which is built on a solid foundation of collaboration will not only reach its intended goals, but exceed them every time.

DON'T CONFORM, STAY TRUE TO YOURSELF

"You'll never make it".

I'm sure many of you have been on the wrong side of that statement.

I have. I still do.

The best way to silence the haters is with achievement.

I'm educated, well-traveled with more than 20 years in my field and still have to prove myself. Not that there's anything wrong with proving yourself, but most of my white male contemporaries are considered to "have arrived". They don't get the line of questioning fueled by ignorance and bias which I so frequently do.

That scenario isn't exclusive to Latinos. African Americans, Asians, women, gay and lesbians, you name it; any member of a minority community comes across these types of prejudiced induced blockers.

The establishment might not say it as plainly as I'm laying it out for you right now, but what they're trying to do is force you to conform, assimilate, stay in your place. Oh they might use carefully crafted words, compliment you, shake your hand, smile at you... maybe even give you a promotion! But beware, the wolf is often dressed in sheep's clothing.

It's imperative that you do your homework. Immerse yourself in the area you wish to work in. That might be researching, learning strategies and making contacts. You have to speak about the subject with authority and authenticity in order for others to pay attention. This isn't a fake it until you make it scenario. Everyone can smell shit a mile away. NOT you. You need to be able to shame the office bully to silence with your sharp and timely marketplace knowledge.

It's imperative to be inquisitive at your workplace. Ask why things are as they are and if there's another way? Nothing drives a stake through the heart of a company than complacency. You have to be the one to drive innovation. That doesn't mean all the great ideas must come from you. Genius is sometimes a cubicle away.

Don't think you're the only frustrated employee. Use those water cooler chats for something more productive than talking about last night's game or the office gossip. You can be a facilitator by networking with other likeminded doers.

Identify who are the influencers in your department or project. These colleagues are not necessarily managers. If you pay close attention, you're sure to identify who are the most well-liked and respected people at your place of work. Titles don't command respect or admiration; people do. In order to get into the decision making house so to speak, you need to focus your effort on getting these human side doors, back doors and windows to understand and believe in your goals. These people are not necessarily the members of your department. They don't even need to join the project, but perhaps they can help beat the drum about it.

You'll know you're on the right path when you and your ideas are being championed by the influencers in a room of decision makers without you being present.

YOU ONLY TAKE WITH YOU WHAT YOU GIVE AWAY

I'm among the fortunate ones who throughout their career have earned the respect of talented, experienced professionals. They selflessly lent me their time and shared their insights, often literally and figuratively opening doors of opportunity.

To that end, I work with many organizations which champion the fair treatment of Latinos. I am a lifetime member of the National Association of Hispanic Journalists (NAHJ) and have served as president. I am a member of the business advisory board for the National Hispanic Media Coalition (NHMC) and I am also on the programming committee for Hispanicize.

I design and lead workshops and panel discussions; frequently as a guest speaker for media related events and classrooms.

I'm also the co-founder of the Latino Multimedia Communicators social media group which shares, discusses and supports professionals and their strategies/products of interest to the Latino community. You can find us on Facebook.

We all need guidance in our lives, whether it's personal, or professional. We need leaders to help us find our way, and not just to pave the way. There are key moments in a person's professional and personal life that we can point to and say, "This was a turning point for me. This was the end of one chapter and the beginning of another." And more often than not there are heroes who help us turn those pages.

Many different journalism organizations have given me the chance to meet a lot of young people, peers and other colleagues in transition. It's always a proud moment to reconnect with someone who I've met early on in their career, or as a student, and then hear them say "I just wanted to let you know the time we spent together made a difference." Whether those conversations were 30-minutes long on giving career advice, or something more involved such as walking them through a period in their career... it was time well invested by me.

Having those people take the time to reach out to you, and share with you, in whatever way you've positively and productively impacted their lives and careers is rewarding because I've had it done for me. As much as a "thank you" is gratifying, the best thank you is to pay it forward and do for others what you've been fortunate enough to have done for you.

STAND UP FOR YOUR COMMUNITY

It is my responsibility to provide a voice to the voiceless. Journalists often forget that it is our constitutional right to question authority and hold the powerful accountable in the pursuit of truth on behalf of the public. Like so many times before, the U.S. presidential election is being used to cast blame on a group of vulnerable people for the social and economic ills that plague this nation.

The use of the term "illegal immigrants", "illegal aliens" and "illegals" in describing people who are in this country without proper documentation is demeaning, inaccurate and disrespectful. It is a propaganda tool used to dehumanize a group of people and instill fear in the general population in order to establish policy.

Right out of the gate, Donald Trump attacked Mexicans during the announcement that he was running for the White House. Soon afterwards I was invited to speak at a television program about how the presidential hopeful was not only alienating the Mexican community, but Latinos in general. Some critics, many Latino – told me that I was wrong. They were quick to correct me that Trump singled out Mexicans and not any other Latino group. That's factually correct of course, but what they failed to see is that for many people in this country we are all the same. Mexicans, Peruvians, Puerto Ricans, fill in the blank for any of the more than 20 Spanish speaking countries... to them, we are all the same.

It is we, the Latinos who don't see how very much alike we are.

Don't get me wrong. I am the first to say that despite the U.S. Census poor attempts to put Latinos in to a nice little bucket labeled U.S. Hispanics; we do not self-describe as such. We don't ask, "Where are you from" because we want to know if you're a Latino. We ask because we want to know where you trace your roots. I am a proud Peruvian-American who recognizes and appreciates that I'm part of a larger family of Latinos in the United States, but that is our community's collective Achilles heel. We celebrate our differences much more than what we have in common. This is why I was chastised for declaring Trump's attack on Mexicans as not only an attack on them, but on all of us. Once again I wasn't "enough".

Who am I to defend the Mexican community? After all, I'm not Mexican or Mexican-American. In some circles I'm not even a real Latino having been born in this country. What do I know about the struggles of immigrants?!

This was the topic of conversation when a friend came calling complaining about the lack of unity among U.S. Latinos and our inability to have a unified front in the fight for fairness, equality, respect. It is difficult to have one voice when there are historical divides between Peruvians and Ecuadorians, Colombians and Venezuelans, Caribbean's and Central-Americans, etc. Except there is one difference; the children of those immigrants.

We, the sons and daughters, many who have been made to feel "not enough" for a number of excuses have the opportunity to declare their own republic forged by the common experiences of second, third and fourth generation Latinos.

We, the children of two worlds don't need to inherit the historical road blocks of our fathers. We can choose to unite to defend the rights of one another, to support causes which affect us directly or by association, to take our place at the decision making table in politics, society and business.

We are proud of the historical revolutionary, innovative, industrious spirit of the United States of America. We build on a solid foundation of family values, strong work ethic and pride instilled in us by our parents. We provide a united voice and offer an open palm in support of one another in times of celebration or trouble.

We can do all those things and much more because what made us different in our youth makes us the same in our formidable years… we are American Latinos.

WELCOME TO THE UNITED STATES, AQUÍ SE HABLA ESPAÑOL

I was shopping with my wife at the Wal-Mart in our Central Connecticut neighborhood when I noticed a curious thing. The employees were putting up new billboard signs identifying the different sections at the mega store… in Spanish. There it was, side by side, a sign which read "Auto Care", "Cuidado para el Automovil". You can argue there's a need for that "se habla español" service in large Latino hubs like Miami or Los Angeles, but Central Connecticut?

The truth is that it's increasingly difficult not to come across Spanish being spoken in the U.S., no matter the market size.

Hablar español en Los Estados Unidos no es un lujo, si no una necesidad.

A recent study by the Instituto Cervantes finds that more people speak Spanish in the United States than anywhere in the world; second only to Mexico. The U.S. Census Bureau estimates that up to 43 million people will be speaking Spanish in 2020. This shouldn't be a surprise given the history that language has had in this country. There are nine states that started off as Spanish colonies. Add on the acquisition of Puerto Rico and the consistent emigration from Latin American countries and well, like I said - it shouldn't be a surprise.

Companies see that the best way to grow their business is to better serve the booming Latino population in their language of choice. Sometimes that's English, sometimes Spanish and sometimes both. With a purchasing power of nearly $1.5 trillion, embracing bilingualism is good for business.

Even-though Latinos are driving the population and economic growth of this country, we are still underrepresented across all industries including newsrooms.

UNCONSCIOUS BIAS: CLONING IN THE WORKPLACE

I'm often the only Latino around a decision-making table.
Nielsen reports that the multicultural population is 120-million strong
and increasing by 2.3 million per year in the United States. They make
up 38 percent of the population today, and are projected to become
the numeric majority by 2044.

According to a *Fortune* magazine 2014 report, more than 95 percent
of Fortune 500 CEOs were white men. If you were to look at their
organizational charts and their direct reports, you would see that all
would be a reflection of them — white men.

How could it be there are so few of "us" and so many of "them" in
top management positions, when study after study shows that the
multicultural community is leading not only the country's population
growth, but also the economic growth as well?

The answer is unconscious bias.

The first criterion that hiring managers use to recruit candidates is
themselves — when measuring skill sets and experience, and when
deciding if the person would be a good fit with the company's culture.
This culture is bred by the "haves," which limits the "have-nots"
because of a lack of shared experiences like socioeconomic factors,
including education.

Homogeneity isn't strictly a white male problem — it applies to
any recruiter who a candidate is facing across the table. Research
by the Kellogg School of Management found that hiring managers
favored recruits who shared their experiences and interests. The
demographic makeup of a company might look diverse, but what's
underneath is the same.

So, how do we break this chain of cloning in the workplace? Well, like patients seeking help with an addiction, executives first need to accept that they have a problem. One can only help leaders who realize that they must embrace and apply a philosophical change.

The fact that I'm a Latino does not pardon me from unconscious bias. As a hiring manager, I make it a point to engage and develop relationships with people from other backgrounds. You can do that in the workplace by inviting colleagues for coffee or lunch. I also travel to various markets across the country, attending events representative of different communities in order to up my game.

As the multicultural market grows, a diverse workforce is key in providing companies with a competitive edge that is vital to their future success. If not corrected, unconscious bias will lead to poor decision-making, and result in a company becoming irrelevant and inevitably obsolete.

GET OFF THE SIDELINES

In order to effect positive change in the workplace, you have to get off your ass and get involved.

The often well intended, but naïve company priority initiatives miss their mark because the persons who lead them aren't diverse themselves. I can't tell you how many arrogant executives speak as if they know better than employees who are part of the target community. While I am a champion of women and African-American issues; I'm not a woman and I'm not African-American. I would never pretend to be the right person to lead initiatives in reaching those two groups. That's not to say that my experience and interest wouldn't be of value in a larger discussion; it's just that the point persons should be representatives of those groups. There are many nuances in developing focused messages which require persons who have firsthand experiences because of their race, age, gender, sexual orientation and other.

It's ironic to me that diversity and inclusion initiatives to provide greater visibility to a community often lack visibility itself. I'm most often part of U.S. Hispanic focused teams. For all the talk about being inclusive and reflective of them; centered content does not get the top billing it deserves. They're placed in forgettable slots reserved for program fillers and are the first to get cut due to time or space constraints. The committees in charge of these initiatives pat themselves on the back for the few bread crumbs that do make it through, but then are bewildered when those tokens do not bear fruit.

For any message to get through it needs frequency. If you're showing up once a year for Hispanic Heritage Month or worse the patronizing, land mine riddled Cinco de Mayo – you lost even before you began.

Any strategy needs frequency in order for its intended audience to notice and understand. Diversity initiatives should not be adopted by companies for a finite time; have expiration dates. They should be standard operating procedure considering the impact diversity has on businesses.

Another reason why diversity initiatives fail is because of a lack of responsibility beginning with the C suite. And it trickles down. The front line cares about what the back office determined as important. There's no greater motivation than to know that diversity initiatives will be part of one's performance review. It's a whole new perspective when an employee understands that their salary increase and promotion are tied to their ability to meet the goals of the company priority. This is how conversations turn into actions.

In order for content to be authentic it requires authors who walk in the shoes of those you're trying to connect with. We aren't telling our stories...they are. Y quienes son ellos para contar nuestras historias? Ellos que no saben nuestro idioma. Ellos que no han sido testigos de los sacrificios of our parents and grandparents or perhaps our own.

How many times am I going to hear, "I can't find talented and experience Latinos for that job? You can't find them? Oye...habré los ojos because you're not looking.

LEADERSHIP TRAITS

Managers are appointed, but leaders are elected. An employer appoints the manager of a department, but that doesn't mean those they manage accept them as a leader. That's a title that needs to be earned over time via developing and nurturing relationships.

Too often managers overuse the word "I" as in "I did this. I accomplished that. My team, my project." I think it's great to have a sense of ownership, but it's also vital to provide opportunities for members of your team to lead. It is critical for their development to be assigned as the point person of projects which provides them greater access and visibility to a company's upper management. It's a symbol of not only recognition and reward, but of confidence in their abilities. The fastest way, from my experience, to advance is to mentor your successor. And the only way to do that is by elevating the members of the team you oversee.

A leader must also take responsibility and be accountable. My philosophy is "I'll take the blame, you take the credit". Too many teams and organizations are risk averse. They're afraid of making mistakes because of the negative consequences. I've never known any successful person in any field that hasn't embraced failure. If a person or a team is to be innovative than it is on the leader to eliminate the insecurity which an environment of adverse repercussions bring. Every achievement I've had in my career has been paved by a long road of errors and I'm all the better for it.

In the end the only real mistake is the one which is made more than once.

AIM SMALL, MISS SMALL

If I could go back in time, I would say to myself "Aim small, miss small".Too often at work as in life we bite off more than we can chew. We set grandiose goals for ourselves like the perennial New Year's resolution of exercising regularly and quickly losing weight. I'm the first to admit my personal promise to lose 30 pounds in 30 days was a perfect example of failing fabulously. I could share with you a laundry list of reasons why it was unrealistic of me to achieve my goal, but at the center was my inability to hyper focus my challenge. It is often the same when setting workplace goals. The only sure results of setting unrealistic stretch goals are stress and frustration.

Stop authoring statements to neatly fit a presentation's title or office lingo. The more detailed your goal is, the better your chances of achieving success. It will become the road map you and your colleagues will use to ask the right questions, evaluate progress and delegate responsibilities.

The intention of using the losing weight example is to provide insights on how to properly frame challenges in order to minimize the chances of failing and optimize the chances to succeed.

So, here is the new challenge: I am going to lose weight by making healthy changes in my lifestyle. I will eat balanced meals regularly and exercise for at least an hour, three times a week. By being faithful to these adjustments in my daily routine, I estimate that I will lose 30 pounds in 4 months.

This challenge is one I can wrap my arms around versus the first Himalayan one I started the year with. Not only is it more realistic, but when I break it down by section the road map to success is laid out for me.

My New Year's resolution catastrophe was in that I wanted to simplify what is in fact very complex. The chore of my goal really wasn't about losing 30 pounds in 30 days; it's about changing my lifestyle.

If you aim small, focus on what you can do based on the resources in front of you and provide a scheduled timetable in which to accomplish it, then you'll miss small.

Expect to make mistakes along the way. The challenges which veered off, but got right back on track were the ones which had easy lane access.

By the way... 3 weeks and 5 pounds. I'm not on course, but I'm also not completely lost.

WRITING A BOOK

One needs to have a certain level of tenacity in reaching their goals. Whatever it is you want to achieve, make sure to dedicate your heart and mind to it because that's what it's going to take.

Writing, collaborating on a book is a goal which provides me with a concrete method of sharing knowledge, because you can touch it, point to it, and even read from it. It is a business card which speaks to the body of your work and what you have a passion for.

My hope is that this book will provide other opportunities to write more books in the future, to collaborate with others on other projects, to open doors for myself and others. I've been very fortunate through my career in media, and through my volunteer work with different organizations to share knowledge and work with many talented people. I see this book as just another platform to be able to continue to contribute.

BIOGRAPHY

WHO AM I?

I'm Hugo Balta.

Hijo de Hugo y Graciela.

Brother to Diana, Monica and Veronica.

Esposo de Adriana.

Isabella and Esteban's Papa.

I'm also grandson to abuelita Hortencia.

It's been more than 10 years since she passed away, but she is never far from me. My grandmother never had the title CEO, President or GM...but she had one title rarely given: abuelita, which as many of you know is very different than abuela.

She never had much of a checking or savings account...but she was rich from the love of her family.

She didn't have any formal schooling...no bachelor, masters or doctorate ...but she had a degree from life...education that is still teaching me today.

She didn't get to see much of the world, but she was worldly...an enlightened human being who knew you don't need to go across the globe to find what's right in front of you.

Courage...ni hablar - at 5'1, she'd stare down any figurative and literal Goliath.

I am family to a few, friend to many and colleague to more than that. I am my own person and the sum of the parts of a generous many including mi abuelita Hortencia. If at any time someone pays attention to Hugo, it is because he is the voice of and for many. It isn't difficult to stand and face the opposition, however great... when you're reassured by the strength and experience of an even greater nation. They might have the power, but we have the numbers y tarde ó temprano por las buenas o las malas change is coming.

CHAPTER THREE

DAMIANO RAIGOZA

Ontological Leadership

Ontology: The study of the nature of being, existing, or reality.

Leadership: The action of leading a group of people or an organization.

> "If you're going to be a leader, you're going to have to have a very loose relationship with this thing you call 'I' or 'me.' Maybe that whole thing in me which the universe revolves isn't so central. Maybe life is not about self but about self-transcendence."
>
> – Werner Erhard

Your natural leadership began long before your heart started to beat. Before you were placed in the hostile environment of the womb, data shows that only one in 14 million sperm would reach the fallopian tubes. In fact, ninety percent of all ejaculated sperm is deformed, says Mayo Clinic. Once a sperm has reached the fallopian tubes and picked up the chemical trails to reach the egg, it penetrates deeply and fertilizes the egg that becomes you. Quick question: Do you think the sperm and egg were worried about what they looked like? No, the sperm and egg did instinctively what they knew to do. Did the sperm worry about getting too far ahead of the other sperm because the other sperm might think he was a show off? Of course not—that's absurd. They were just "being." You've been a sexy swimmer that leads since the day you left your father's testicles.

During the first trimester of fetal development, week five is when your brain, spinal cord, heart, and other organs began to form. In week six your heart started to pump blood. Each of us is a beautiful miracle. We were all born leaders and became great when our seed was planted, the day we were conceived. Nine months later you were born; if there were complications, you got through them and are here today to read these thoughts, so right on!

The intention of this chapter is to remind you of your natural self-expression in leadership just like when you were a sperm that reached the egg. My promise is to give this chapter my all like Kobe Bryant gave in his last game as a Los Angeles Laker in 2016. Here's to leaving it all on the court.

When you are in the zone, on the court playing a sport, you don't necessarily think about how to shoot a basketball, swing a bat, or kick a ball; you just "are." The sperm was just "being" and took action and swam and became you. What we can learn from your very first leadership experience is that you took action. It consisted of you having stamina, of pushing yourself to have the energy to complete the task. Thus, **our first effective leadership principal is to take action and have the stamina to finish what you started.**

I was born February 15, 1978, in Lynwood, California at St. Francis Hospital. I came home to an apartment in Cudahy, California, which is approximately ten miles south east of downtown Los Angeles. Cudahy is predominantly populated by Latino immigrants and in the 1980s, Cudahy was infested with major gangs. It's where I learned to be a leader.

I was eight and my two older brothers were fifteen and sixteen when I started to follow them around like a puppy dog, happily wagging its tail. It was on these adventures that I developed a great deal of life experience and learned how to connect with people much older than myself, from all walks of life. **Another principal of being an effective leader is to connect with and build relationships, alliances, and support with other human beings.**

Other people are resources for our lives. Abraham Maslow's hierarchy of needs claims that the most basic of these needs are: friendship, love, security, and intimacy. These are why many kids like myself join gangs: because of a sense of belonging. Other kids get it from playing sports or being part of church groups and private country clubs; some have great family structure and bonding at home. While my little mother did her very best to provide for my two brothers and me by herself, growing up, I joined a tagging and break dancing crew to be a part of something bigger than myself. This crew had leaders that I looked up to. There was "Willie Survive" who was skilled in dancing, "Magic" the spray can artist, "Capone" who got people to listen, and "Cottna" and "PeeWee" who made more money than the chief of police. I learned leadership traits in this setting like confidence, taking action, and listening before I speak. Yet I also embraced traits that did not function in the long run, like taking things personally and a fear that everyone was out to get me.

An effective leader knows that everyone wants to be noticed and accepted. We all have written on our foreheads: "acknowledge me" and "say something nice to me." It's a basic need we all have as humans. Babies will actually die from lack of touch, shutting down the hormone and immune systems because of a lack of love (which has been the case in orphanages). As a powerful leader, you must first understand and "get" another human being—understand who they are and who they are not, then start to see their greatness. Recognition is the master motivator and when you do this, you create people who you want, and you create a new future. Understand that everyone alive won the race and fertilized the egg. Appreciate people for living this experience called "life." Everyone wants to live an amazing life. As an effective leader, you must connect with others in such a way that they are empowered by being in your presence. **Effective leadership recognizes the power of acknowledgement.**

Let's take a moment to look at the makeup of our minds and a portion of its function. When you were born, there weren't many experiences recorded in the brain. As you started to live outside your mother's womb, your brain started recording everything it saw, heard, felt, smelled, and tasted up through the spinal cord, past the reticular activating system (RAS), also known as the read and scan part of your brain, and stored it. Over the years you experienced "events." These events, whether good or bad, were actually neutral. Yet the experience caused you to record it with feelings and emotions, and then you added your created story to the event. As you grew older, the brain scanned for similarities in your situations in order to create a reaction so that you would survive, and be safe. These experiences created a belief system that kept getting validated.

For example, say you raised your hand in elementary school and asked a question to get clarity on a subject, yet a little boy yelled out, "That's a stupid question" and the other kids laughed. What may have happened was your body tensed up, you got sweaty, your heart started palpitating, and you told yourself right then and there, "I'm never going to ask questions again because I could die!"

Now imagine that there's a guy named John sitting in the RAS part of your brain. He watches everything that happens to you, and when he sees something that threatens his (your) existence, he sounds an alarm. He makes sure that you play it safe, be quiet, run, hide. He's the one who reminds you to cross the street when you see a shady character walking toward you.

I invite you to question your fears, question your beliefs, question your ways of being, and see if they were inherited from watching someone else like your parents, your culture, or something you made up. Dig deep into the life you have created up until now, question yourself, and write down your authentic answers. Start to look at the people you are leading—who have you attracted in your life? Ask yourself, Where am I being mediocre in my leadership? The leaders you look up to, what are their ways of being, and how do they act? How do you currently train others as a leader—are you like a professional athlete? **An effective leader is in the question, seeking a bigger question.**

I know we like answers, but ask yourself another question. Stand on a question and look out from on top of that question and look for a bigger question. I invite you to keep seeking, learning, and growing because thoughts become things and help effective leaders know themselves.

Try it on like a coat: your thinking has an effect on your physiology, how you stand, sit, walk, talk, shake hands, etc. **Being an effective**

49

leader is a state of mind and physiology. Do me a favor: sit up like an effective leader. Now, I bet you stood up straight, shoulders back, chest high, head up. Now try on the physiology of a loser. I can imagine your body drooping over like you feel when you get a flat tire. Our internal state drives our performance. Does your physiology beam confidence and power? Notice the people you lead. Start to notice their posture as well as your own. Posture can be a clue to how people are thinking. Crossed arms may indicate skepticism, doubt, being closed off, tired, or simply being cold. Paying attention to your surroundings, to people, to emotions, and receiving feedback can help you create velocity in your life and in those you lead.

Another aspect of our state of mind is our **awareness** and paying attention to the details in the moment. This is a gift that all effective leaders reflect on. Being aware and understanding the power of **now**: what's the best use of my time *now*, what can I focus on right *now*, what can I appreciate right now, who's in front of me now. All I have in life or I will ever have is only now, in the moment.

Authenticity, being real, is a powerful characteristic of an effective leader. Be someone who acts consistently and congruently with who you say you are. As I grew up with kids much older than me, I always wanted to prove myself. I did the craziest things to get approval and to look tough. I developed the nickname "Killer Bee." I got beat up by teenagers in the tagging crew when I was nine and was told that if I cried, I couldn't join the crew. After being beaten for 18 seconds by four teenagers, we celebrated and laughed it off. What developed from this experience was the need to survive, to look tough, to be liked and accepted. My brain was rewired from this experience and it's how I lived most my young life. I wasn't being my true self. I was a good kid that naturally liked others, but I numbed myself and to look tough, I scared other kids walking through my neighborhood with, "Hey, where you from?" Imagine a twelve-year-old running up to you with guts and conviction asking you where you're from and saying that you had better get out of their neighborhood because you didn't belong there. All this to get a little pat on the back, like a puppy getting stroked by his master. These thinking patterns would later bring me to my knees in pain, sorrow, and a dysfunctional life. **All leaders go through experiences that test their identity and leave them with reinventing themselves.**

I joined the United States Navy shortly after being in San Bernardino county jail for six months. Joining the Navy was an adventure. Physically, boot camp was a cinch. I've been an athlete my whole life and it was like a fun obstacle. Yet mentally it was a challenge because I took things personally and didn't like being told what to do. Because I excelled at the physical training and got up earlier than the rest of the recruits to train with the Navy Seal Buds program, I was honored by my drill instructors. It was in the marching with very little sleep, pulling together teams, and going through the experience with my shipmates that I began to reinvent myself and my identity. I started to realize that there was much more to life than the one I was living. I started to realize that my mom was right: "Birds of a feather flock together." My new friends were from Louisiana, Indiana, and Florida. I began to reinvent my identity. What the military gave me was **discipline**, which is another principal of being an effective leader. Discipline is the motor of the vehicle that gets you to your results. The vehicle is the career you choose. Do you have a Ferrari type of discipline or a four banger that has engine problems?

While serving in the United States Navy I had many examples of men and women who were the epitome of **integrity**. They did what they say they were going to do, the way it was meant to be done, even if no one was looking. Integrity is the foundation of building an empire that will stand the test of time. In terms of integrity, I mean being complete. Being complete is a powerful stance to create from. The people that volunteer to follow you do so because you possess this trait. You will create the impossible, move mountains, and things that never moved before will now move because of your commitment to do what you say. The stand that you take will create a force, an energy, that will line you up with the highest vibrations of the universe and will be the key that unlocks closed doors for everyone else.

As you become the person you imagine, filled with skills beyond measure—a master—living in the context of a leader's life can start to diminish if there is one variable that is not exercised. All the hard work and accomplishments can start to feel in vain, useless, and futile. This one variable is **contribution**. Fulfillment is felt when you give your time and energy to supporting others in reaching their goals. Zig Ziglar says, "When you help enough people reach their goals, you'll reach yours." A leader gets involved, coaches, teaches, trains, mentors, and inspires others. When you live for yourself, your goals, and your desires, you live a small life of deception. Ultimately, I say it comes down to effective duplication. Can you create a system that's duplicable and simple enough that others can do it themselves?

Lastly, **leadership is a context of living.** Context is an unseen point of view of the world that you believe. The context in which I live my life is abundance, and abundance shows up in my business, love, relationships, and lifestyle. Start to see the context that you are living from. Like a fish: it doesn't see the water, isn't necessarily aware of the water, yet everything in the fish's world is surrounded by the fact that it exists in water.

Consider that everything that shows up in your life, like your thoughts, feelings, and relationships, is consistent with the context from which you live. The context of your life creates the content of your life and gives it meaning (an excerpt from one of my many mentors, John Hanley). In the context of responsibility, and acting from this mindset, an effective leader knows he or she can count on themselves no matter what shows up in life. Living from this point of view, an effective leader who is responsible for all that he or she creates, realizing that they are the cause of events rather than living from a victim's point of view (as being abandoned, stranded, and helpless) truly puts them in a position to win consistently. Make a commitment to learn, grow, risk, and master circumstances. Make the mantra become "molehills vs. monstrous mountains." What gets created in you after becoming an effective leader is freedom and full self-expression.

Today, I am a corporate trainer, life coach, and have run a successful mortgage business for the last 12 years. I also buy and hold, flip, and sell real estate. What I am most excited about is working closely with my wife and building our business together.

Damiano O. Raigoza

BIOGRAPHY

Coach Damiano is a leading trainer, seminar designer, corporate consultant and founder of Success Education Coaching and Seminars. He is dedicated to creating exceptional business results. He partners with his clients to design and implement organizational initiatives that produce significant, sustainable change in a surprisingly short period of time. His commitment is to use all the professional tools and assets available to help you live powerfully and to love the life you live. Coach Damiano has delivered training and consulting programs to such business as: Century 21, Re/Max, Coldwell Banker, Realty One Group, International City Mortgage, New York Life, Mass Mutual, Bellagio Wealth Corp and many private businesses with an emphasis and niche on self-employed entrepreneurs creating a paradigm shift in business building and velocity in team thinking. He is most proud of his wonderful wife and children

CHAPTER FOUR

ROLANDO CASTRO

TRUE LEADERSHIP BEGINS FROM WITHIN

> "If your action inspire others to dream more,
> learn more and become more, you are a leader"
>
> – John Quincy Adams

Born the second of five boys in our family; I grew up in the city of Lynwood. My Dad went to work and my mother was a stay home mom. I grew up with clothes on my back and a roof over our head, life was amazing.

I have an older brother Manny who is a year and a half older than me. I have a younger brother Jerry who passed away in 2006; he was about a year younger than me. I have two younger brothers Fernando and Andy. We grew up with much testosterone; it drove my mom crazy at times. As a kid growing up, life was truly fantastic. I cannot complain about the way I grew up and how our parents raised us.

As a child, I would discover that I was very analytical. I would always want to know what the average of things was. If we were going somewhere, I would calculate how long it would take. First, I'll calculate how many miles, and then I'd figure out how long it will take us to get there.

I always had a passion for money; my dad would give us a $1.00 allowance every week, and I would love to calculate how things work with relation to money. If I wanted to buy something, I'd figure out how many hours I had to work to get it. I would always catch myself mentally working numbers, back the I never understood why. As I grew older, I became interested in knowing how things worked. Why did things happen? I knew there had to be a reason behind it. During my formative years, I did not pay attention to this stuff, but as I went to junior high and high school, I developed that curiosity and needed to know why.

My entrepreneur spirit comes from my father. He worked for a company for many, many years. Then in 1998, he decided to open a clothing store, a family-owned business. The business was in the same city where we lived. He went and bought clothes wholesale and sold it at retail. Of all the brothers, I was the one that worked in that business. No other sibling but me; I do not know why. I would work on the weekends and after school. Knowing we had a business to run and a job to fulfill, there was rarely any time to go hang out with my friends. Instead, I worked in the family business.

My dad's first business venture was doing so great that he decided to quit his job which resulted in being a huge mistake. He lacked the understanding of where his success was coming from or why his business was doing so great. All he knew was that he wanted to be there and grow his business full time.

After about a year into the business, we bought our first home in the City of Lynwood. My dad surprised my mother with the new house and till this date, I will never forget the look on my mom's face when she saw the house my dad bought her. She began to cry; she did not like the house at all. I guess her vision of her first home would have been in a better neighborhood as well as a much bigger house. However, after a while, my mother got used to it and soon enough she began to call it her home.

My dad is the kind of person that loves to give, loves to help out people. Unfortunately, people took advantage of that. With the amount of success, he was obtaining with his business; he developed the wrong kind of friends. My dad believed them to be friends, but they were only around because he had more money than them and would often buy them things. I am a big believer that you are the average of the five people you hang around with, and my dad was a clear testament to that statement being accurate. His friends were not the best of people; they had bad habits such as over excessive drinking and constantly abusing drugs. That is when my dad developed the habit of drinking more than he normally would and eventually began to use drugs, I guess it was his way of fitting in with his friends.

Our family business lasted about 18 months, and it was primarily due to the lack of understanding how to run a successful business, and I can honestly say that my dad's drinking and bad behavior lead to us having to shut it down for good. So, during that dark episode of seeing my dad develop a drinking habit, losing our family business, we also lost our very first place we called home. In 18 months, we lost everything. At that time, I did not understand why I only knew that we were in a place I wish to never relive again.

One morning, my dad found himself without a job since and for a few years we found ourselves moving from place to place and in many instances having to live with family members. My dad had a hard time finding work, since no one wanted to hire him, he decided to hire himself and went into the construction business and created Delya's Construction which was named after my niece. During the time when my father began his new venture, I can recall working up to 4 jobs so that I could support my family. One thing that I am proud of was never being upset at having to work so many jobs, I only knew that this experience is not permanent and one-day things will eventually get better.

My dad being that person who refuses to give up, he promised us one day things will get better and that our future lays upon his level of leadership. I recall at times waking up late at night for a glass of water; I would always see my dad reading and studying books about architecture, reading blue prints and building homes. He would go through an entire book in English in less than one week. In my guess, he read at least a dozen book and the day came when he said; I am launching another business, and the business will be construction. He had no physical experience but did acquire a wealth of knowledge by reading all those books, and was now willing to put his skills (theoretically) to the test. I had a job at the time, and again he invited me to work for the family business. A big part of me did not want to; I was not looking forward to waking up at 5 am and walk around with a hammer and look for stuff to smack but being that team player that I am, I said okay, let's do it. Next, we were on our way to developing the new family business.

A year in, business was great, it felt my dad was onto something with this construction thing. To be honest, I did not enjoy working in that type of field, it was not my thing, I was always afraid of it. The one thing my dad would say is, "If you are scared of a hammer, you are going to get hurt." Moreover, I was always frightened of walking on roofs, hammering nails and stepping on a nail or two.

This business lasted about four years or so. Unfortunately, my dad once more attracted the wrong friends, made a lot of bad business decisions that jeopardized our cash flow and overall business. Right around 2008 when the market began to crash, my dad's second business came crashing down and yes the market crash played a huge role, but the decisions he made played a major role why we could not save the business.

Looking back at both experiences my dad had with his businesses, as I write this I am 34 years old and just now old realized why his businesses did not thrive. Now I understand the type of mistakes he made and how his decision affected the future of his business as well as the future of his family. I wish I would have understood then what I do now, maybe I could have made a difference but things happen for a reason and looking back, there is nothing I would change as each of those lessons has shaped me to the entrepreneur I am today.

I honestly believe that my dad made those mistakes, went through those tribulations with two failed businesses in a way to teach me a lesson. I was being equipped psychologically without knowing that, one day, I will run and operate my own business. Maybe I am wrong; maybe I am crazy for wanting to believe that my dad made those mistakes, sacrificed his future so that one day I can apply to those same lessons in my own business. To this date, every decision that I make I think about my dad and I ask myself if it will ultimately help me or will it hurt me. Unconsciously my dad is in business with me every day because the lesson he taught me are engraved in me so deep that I will never forget them.

LEADERSHIP

I believe leadership is important nowadays because, with social media being a part of our life, we are easily influenced by somebody else's lifestyle. We know that with social media, there is a lot of huff and puff about the realities of how things are. Half of that stuff is not even real; but some people want to portray a role that they are better than someone, that they are somebody that they are obviously not. That might influence someone to take action. Many people act on impulse rather than strategy because they want to be like that person. You cannot afford to be influenced by what other people are doing; we cannot compare our chapters with theirs.

I can honestly say that I am guilty of that sometimes. If I see somebody that looks to be successful or has achieved something I wish to accomplish, I can get desperate at times and catch myself comparing myself to that person. I begin to ask myself "Why am I not there?" Moreover, then I am like, "Wait a minute, I do not know what their story is" or, sometimes, we are moved by what people are doing. We want to do those things because it is cool, it influences us. Leadership is essential because you have to know and understand what your values are, what you want, what your purpose in life is.

A great leader must understand the first person they lead will be themselves. Leaders are not influenced by what other people do nor are they motivated by what other people say. If we are unable to lead ourselves, if we are influenced by what other people are doing, we do not understand what leadership is all about and will forever be following the wrong leaders.

LEARNING LEADERSHIP QUALITIES

My leadership moment came when I was fresh out of high school which was in 1999 graduating from Lynwood High School. I do not have much of a college education; I went to school for massage therapy which I graduated with honors. I went to a few city colleges but honestly, school was not for me, and it goes back to my circle of influence. I was hanging out with friends who were not inspired; they did not have big goals of accomplishing great things, and because I lacked leadership skills, I too was not inspired nor was I motivated to continue my education and pursue a career worth having.

As I grew older and was on my way to becoming a man, I was forced to take on the responsibility to become the leader of my family. As I mentioned before regarding the experience I shared with my dad, the unfortunate events where he drank a lot, and abusing drugs, my father found himself in a very dark place. I had no choice but to step up as the man of the house mainly because my older brother had moved out because he became the leader of his family.

I recall being in my late teen's early twenties, I worked 3 to 4 jobs at a time to support my family. We were moving from place to place because I could not afford to keep up with the bills on my income alone; I could only afford to pay so much for rent and utilities. My dad would have his good moments where we would stay in one place for a while. Then, he would have his bad moments, where we had to move out because I could not afford the house payments. I had to take a leadership role in regards to being the sole provider for my family.

In 2006, our family suffered one of the biggest blows we have ever received, my younger brother Gerardo was murdered, and that is something that till now almost ten years later have not been able to recover from. At that time, I had two younger brothers to look after, and the loss of my brother caused both my mother and father to go into a depression. Not understanding why this happened to us, why would GOD take our brother from us when we needed him the most when we were in a stage of vulnerability and did not know how to handle his loss. I knew my family needed me the most, I was in charge of my two younger brothers, my mother, and my father's welfare. A leader was born right then and there; I knew the future of my family began with the quality of person I needed to become.

I accepted the leadership role because I needed a better future, the issues at home were such that I could only control them to some limited extent. My surroundings, aside from my home life, I was able to control. I chose to read; I decided to search for inspiration, to find motivation. Not once did I complain about the role I had to play as a young adult. I only knew it was going to get better. That is when my leadership was born; I needed to lead myself out of that environment I was in into something better.

Fast forward, I am now 34 years of age, I have a mentor who's a great friend of mine. His name is Gary Chomiak. We've been working with one another for four years. I also have a business coach that helps me with the development of my current business; his name is Charlie Lowe. I've been meeting with him consistently every month for the past four years, Gary and Charlie play a significant role in the success that I have achieved thus far.

THREE STRATEGIES LEADERS SHOULD HAVE

Three strategies that I believe every leader should have: One is humility. I feel that a real leader genuinely cares about other people, deeply cares about making an impact on the people that he is leading, and understands that the people he is leading can someday be their own leaders. I met many leaders that take their leadership role for granted, or they often take it to heart where they only want to lead and don't really focus on developing leaders. I believe a real leader understands that their role is not only leading others to his or her goals but to help his/her followers reach their goals as well. I know that is important for me.

One thing I always tell my employees is "You might not work for my company forever; I am aware of that. However, while you are here, I am going to make sure I give you the skills needed that if one day you decide to leave my company and some other company hires you, they will be getting the perfect employee". Because of that, I feel that I am a great leader. They always give me their 100 percent because I provide them with the opportunity to become leaders themselves.

My goal is for my employee to become better people and when you are a better person, you live a better lifestyle; you are happier, you develop the confidence to face the challenges this crazy world brings us every day. When something arises, you are ready for it; you are prepared. By providing them with those skills, they become the best employees any employer can ever have. A leader has to understand it is not always about leading; it is about creating leaders as well.

Another trait that I feel that leaders need to have is they must be visionaries. I feel that as a leader, your job is to create a vision for the future you want to create for yourself, and for others. It is not always just about me and what I want in my business, I have my goals; I have objectives that I want to accomplish, and my employees are going to help me to reach my goals. However, what about their goals? They come to work; they work their butts off here for me. My vision is not just for me; it is for them as well. A big part of my job is to find out what their goals in life are. What do they want to achieve in life? How can I help you get there? Why? Because you are helping me to achieve my vision. If I create a vision for the company, that means I also have a vision for my personal life. If I give them the skills, they need to do their job to their best of their ability; then they will eventually help me reach my goals. However, in return, as a leader it is my duty to do everything in my power to help them reach their dreams and goals.

BIGGEST FAILURE

My biggest failure in business happened when I opened my second location and failed to understand who my target market was in my business. I was quick to opened the second location without doing my due diligence of why I was doing it if there was a real need for me to do so. It was opened inside of a strip mall that had a lot of foot traffic, I believed people will be lining up to do business with me. I did not understand who my target market was, and it was a huge mistake and a huge loss for me. My target market is not your average consumer; it is the particular customer who needs to take action and purchase my services. Not understanding my target market, not doing my research, I lost a lot of money opening a second location. In actuality, my biggest failure was the biggest lesson I've ever learned in business. You have to take the time to understand who your target market is and how can you cater to that market.

Life's best lessons are learned through trial and error; many people read failure stories in books and magazines, but until you live it yourself, go through the emotions, the embarrassment, what are people are going to think of you. If you do not care about any of those things, then you simply brush it off and say, "You know what, it is fine. Where's the next failure? I am alive; I did not lose anyone by encountering that failure. I am healthy, let's do it." Failure equals success. I am a big believer in that.

UNPLUGGED

I created The Entrepreneur Unplugged for the sole purpose of being able to showcase real people, like you and I, who have real backgrounds and overcame failures, who overcame tribulations, who lost loved ones, and still have a passion for life. I see many people via different social media outlets that are too busy showcasing their successes. Whether it is real or not, it does not matter; it is visible online, not everyone talks about their failures or would want to show you their scars. Many people do not want to let you know that they failed in some aspect of their life.

My goal with Entrepreneur Unplugged is to be able to sit down with someone, interview them where we can talk about their failures in hopes their story can inspire one person that can relate to their story and to pursue their dreams. People say that the best way to success is through failure. However, that can be expensive. The best way is to observe and learn from somebody else's mistakes. My ultimate goal with The Entrepreneur Unplugged is for one day someone who was inspired by a story comes up to me and tells me because of that video, because of a specific story they are now pursuing their goals and living a better quality of life. Every guest on my show shared wonderful stories, events that I would have never thought were possible, and I have been inspired to continue pursuing my goals and set bigger ones as well. Hopefully, my videos inspire the next entrepreneur, who says "Wait a minute, if that person was able to overcome those challenges, so can I" and they take action, they believe in themselves one more time.

I always like to end my show with the following saying, "if our meeting can inspire even one person if just one person says "I am inspired," then our meeting was a success. That is what The Entrepreneur Unplugged is all about. It is about interviewing real people, with real challenges, and showcase how they overcame them.

ON BEING REMEMBERED

I want to be remembered as a person who never gave up. A kid from the City of Lynwood, who might be 34 years old but still has a kid in him. A person who was not afraid to dream big. I would also like to be remembered as someone who took a risk, who believed in himself, and took on enormous challenges, and made something of himself in hopes of inspiring others to do the same. Of course, in the process, I would love to leave a legacy for my children as well. I believe a legacy is more important, more valuable than currency. Last but not least, I want to be remembered as a great husband to my beautiful wife Blanca whom I owe so much to her for making into the man that I am today. She is my rock; she is the person who challenges me every single day to become better than I was yesterday. I love you, Blanca Sandoval.

If somebody would like to sit down and have coffee, pick my brain a little, or just learn more about how I can help them, feel free to shoot me an email to rolando@entrepreneurunplugged.tv If you would like to subscribe to my video blog, please visit

www.entrepreneurunplugged.tv. My website is filled with many resources that can help you on your entrepreneurial journey.

My final thoughts: Never be afraid to dream big. Life is not meant only to be alive; it is intended to be lived. I encourage you to find what your purpose in life is and live life on purpose with a purpose, because at the end; "Success is A Choice."

BIOGRAPHY

Rolando is an influencer and video podcast host of the growing popular show "Entrepreneur Unplugged" At a young age he found himself at the helm of both of his fathers businesses and had to learn with pure instinct and common sense. The valuable lessons he absorbed during this time of his young and impressionable life, he took this experience and opened his very own successful family business with his incredible wife. He considers himself a simple man that grew up in the colorful city of Lynwood, California. Rolando is Self educated and well loved by his peers and employees, and is dedicated to his wife and his beautiful children.

CHAPTER FIVE
REY III VIQUEZ

EMPLOYING SPIRITUALITY IN THE WORKPLACE
LEARNING HOW TO LEAD YOUR MIND BEFORE YOU LEAD OTHERS

Sometime ago, I learned that in order to lead others, the first thing I was going to have to do was to learn to lead my own mind. Following is the story of my journey in discovering the power of the mind, the tactics and tools I used to accomplish a life of gratitude and joyful success.

So let me start with some background. I share this difficult times so that anyone finding themselves in a similar situation can hopefully see a way out through my story.

I own an architectural and interior design company in Los Angeles. After having been in business for a few years, I found myself and my company struggling. When I say struggling I mean to the point that I would pay everyone their paychecks, pay vendors, pay the rent, and I would barely have any money to put gas in my car. In addition to that,

I found myself exhausted and completely wiped out. Life was a series of problems, one after another. There were problems internally within my team, including employees that were problematic; externally we were experiencing very difficult clients and very difficult ongoing project situations. One morning I woke up completely fed up and I said to myself, "either this changes or you close this joint down and go get yourself a job at an architecture firm where you will have a workstation, steady projects and a steady paycheck,"which isn't the life I had envisioned for myself. I felt alone in an imaginary ocean of negativity. While I wasn't alone in life, I must say there is only so much that family and friends can take after a while. That low point, that moment when I hit rock bottom, was truly my tipping point and is the moment when I realized that the one thing missing in my life was a spiritual practice. A faith in a force bigger than myself. A resource that I could feel empowered by or that I could recur to in these seemingly endless difficult times.

NLP: THE FIRST STEP IN MIND DISCOVERY

In establishing the need for a Spiritual practice or resource, let me establish that although I was raised Catholic, I am not a religious person. This story is not at all about religion, but rather spirituality. The first steps I took in seeking that practice, and better life and success for myself and my company, was to engage in studies of Neuro Linguistic Programming. Which is the study of the mind and the language to access the mind.

This was, at the time, exactly what I needed. In learning the NLP system, I began to understand the different types of mind (Visual, Auditory, Logic and Kinesthetic), and how the language that folks use, when you listen to it carefully, will help you determine the type of mind that they come from. This understanding is crucial in my

70

profession, where I am designing a future vision and "selling it" to my clients, my vendors, my team, and people as diverse as life itself. To understand not only how my own Visual mind works and what language makes it tick, but also being able to understand how the minds of others work through the language they use, is an incredibly powerful tool you have at your fingertips. The magic in this tool is knowing how to utilize well... NLP will give you the capability to select the language you use in order to connect with others whose minds work very differently than yours. It really allows you to understand the energy you are working with, and how to shape it to get what you are looking for. I will get into this later in the chapter.

In the meantime, let's just say that after that first day of classes at NLP, I had a client meeting that afternoon, and I walked out and made my first big sale in months. I employed the tactics they began to teach me regarding language, including both verbal and body. I consciously engaged in listening and understanding the person in front of me, and it all worked amazingly in my favor. This was a breakthrough day for me and truly the beginning of a great journey.

At NLP, I learned all about the power of the mind, the most powerful tool we own. I learned how to use it in such a way that I would lead myself, as well as others, into great success. Additionally, I learned the power of Meditation, which I see as a way to access the boundless internal resources that we have been given, All of this was encompassed by the Law Of Attraction (LOA), which I began to study subsequently with my studies of NLP. Without getting too technical, let me just say they all have one overall message: We are the products of our thoughts, our thoughts shape our energy and our behavior which shapes our world. What we think is what we are, and what we think is what our life is and becomes. Our thoughts inform our energy and our energy informs our world. The more you know your mind patterns, your thought patterns, your instincts and the more you know how to use them, the better success you will have in life. In learning this I changed radically, almost immediately as I engaged in a practice of daily Meditation and Mindfulness in my daily life. I also learned to listen very carefully to folks to determine where they were coming from and I began to select the words I used in order to be able to receive the outcome I was looking for. My life went from an ocean of worry to being one of joy and peace. I had been so busy worrying that I was not even paying attention to what was in front of me and how I could take advantage of it. The moment I learned to do that, life became great fun. My thoughts began to change and I began to attract better things for myself.

DOING THE INNER WORK REQUIRED TO DO GREAT OUTER WORK

They say that in order to change your life, you must change your point of view of your life. I say that in order to change your point of view of your life, you must change your point of view of yourself. In my case I realized I had a lot of work to do on myself in order to change that internal point of view. There was a lot of clean up to do in my internal world. It was truly intimidating and very scary.

So I engaged in a rigorous Meditation practice, where I meditated twice a day. Once in the morning the moment I got up for 20 minutes, and once at night, before going to bed for another 20 minutes.

The power of that stillness and silence in my life created a powerful sense of serenity and ability to have faith that all would be well. For someone like me that had been living for 45 years in constant noise, with a constant chattering mind full of self-judgement, worry, stress and lack, this newfound stillness in Meditation became a resource of abundance. I read many books on Meditation at the time that guided me into different kinds of Meditations. One of the Meditations asked you to imagine being 5 years old and what would you tell that 5 year old kid now. I found myself in tears having gone back to that time in my life and been able to soothe the child within me. Throughout this process, I was doing an internal cleansing of all the junk I had been storing in my own mind. All the beliefs, the former notions, the limiting thoughts I had been carrying with me were now being washed out by Meditation. At times it was messy and uncomfortable, often it was down right painful, but it was so worth every single moment of it. In fact, it was necessary for me in order to gain the clarity and the access that I needed to tap into and cleanse what I call my internal resources. Since I've been able to access them with clarity, I have discovered them to be strong and unlimited.

Meditation gave me the peacefulness I needed, and the access to my internal self, which I discovered contained resources of thought, ideas, solutions and inventions. Prior to this access, I had no idea I had these powerful tools within me. My behavior started to change, I became more forgiving of myself and of others, and definitelymoreselfcon fi dent than I used to be. I began to see the abundance of the universe. I would sit in my patio and mediate before work and I began to hear the sounds of the birds, the leaves ru fflingfeethebreezeandappreciate the light. I felt joy and appreciation for life, that simple. Simultaneously, my outer world started to receive a major cleansing. Old friends, clients and acquaintances that loved being miserable and toxic, started to pull away because they longer had company in me. The changes can be painful but when you look at the big picture of what is happening you realize they are all blessings. They are all leading you to that great new way to see and live life, and I came to find that consistency is the key. Just like working out that the gym to condition your body, it is crucial to maintain consistency in your Meditation practice in order to condition your mind to success.

While Meditation helped me clean the slate to start fresh, Gratitude gave me the way to replace the negative with the positive, the lack with the abundant, the painful with the joyful. I began a daily Gratitude practice of writing down 10 things I was grateful for after my

morning meditation session before leaving the house. That alone can change your life. If you wake up stressed out about the day ahead, the issues you have to resolve on that day, and you stop yourself before leaving the house and write down 10 things you are grateful for, your day is already beginning on a positive note. It opens the doors for you to be able to see the beauty in all things, including the struggle. Participating in this practice daily will assist in completely changing your life into one of abundance and optimism.

For me, the changes were immediate and radical. I used to read about that and at firstnotbelieveit,butthemomentIchangedmy perception of who I was, my behavior changed instantly. The moment I found faith in the universe, my world changed instantly. And others in the external world began to respond to me very differently,andit became clear that those around me were purely a reflectionof myself. I began to see change in everyone as I realized that change had to come from my own perception. Those who wanted to keep misery as company began to fall by the wayside as my energy became renewed and refreshed. I was now a positive force, rather than carrying any negative energy for others to feed off of. Much like The Secret, I realized I would attract the energy that I put out into the world.

EMPLOYING SPIRITUALITY IN THE BUSINESS WORLD

With my spiritual practice my whole world changed drastically for the better and gave me the tools to lead my own mind, and therefore the capability to lead others. I did not just keep my spiritual practice at home, but rather I allowed it to permeate into all aspects of my daily life. I utilized this new force in human interactions, and learned how to use it in the business world as well.

The essential thing I have learned in my Spiritual practice, is the difference between the Spirit and the Ego. When I learned that we all belong to the same big ball of energy that is this wonderful universe that we live in, I realized that was being in touch with the Spirit.[1] It became clear that everything we touch, see and hear is nothing but energy, including ourselves, and that we all belong to that same source of energy. My faith and belief in the Spirit has been the access to abundance that has helped provide me with this new, great life.

Contrary to the Spirit is the Ego. The Ego is limiting, it tries to isolate you, it makes you defensive, it comes from a place of lack rather than abundance, and it is the tool that many corporations use to create a sense of deficiencyinordertoincreasecompetitionandambitionin its employees. Unfortunately, when we are not in touch with Spirit, we are most likely operating under the influence of the Ego.

Therefore we worry. We think there is not enough, and we want to get defensive and fight for what little we think we can get. For me, I do not see these as the traits of a true leader, but rather a person in desperation.

The moment that you understand how to shift your behavior and your belief system from the Ego to the Spirit is the moment you are leading your own mind and you are therefore leading others to come and succeed with you.

Let me give you one example on how I use this knowledge in my daily practice:

I have a client that I have had for many years, and he or she (shall remain genderless and be called "they") can be difficult. They will send me an email, grilling me on the cost of a product, a set of furniture pieces I am trying to sell to them, as well as the payment terms, even though this is a client I have had for years and we have had these discussions plenty of times.

My initial reaction to the email is to be annoyed and immediately retaliate, the moment I stop and I take inventory of my thought process, and I recognize that my Ego is in full force. The Ego wants nothing but to write back and tell this client how ridiculous they are being, but I realize that if I do that, I am just alienating myself, and I would be feeding my ego, and not much would be accomplished.

Instead, I decide to recur to Spirit, hard as it is at the moment. I might have to take 5 minutes of stillness to clear my head, and then I remember that both my client and I belong to the same world of plenty, of abundance, of unlimited possibility and kindness. I also recur to Gratitude, and I realize how grateful I am to this client for their business and for the opportunity they have given me many times in the past. I also recognize that they are coming from their own Ego and their sense of lack, pressure, etc. And that's the moment I decide to respond with a kind email that has grateful energy and explain what I've been requested to explain. With the understanding that we both belong to one world, one universe, one project, and one big ball of energy, I am kind while I still maintain the original terms of the agreement/estimate. Key element here, I maintain the same terms of the agreement and hold my ground, something that my Meditation practice has given me, a strong self confidence, and commitment to my business needs and my terms. My spiritual practice has given me a self love and a faith in myself that has brought a way to lead my business and my team to a work environment of joy and commitment to excellence.

The next day I receive an email from my clients assistant letting me know that the estimate has been approved, and a check has been processed and it is on its way to my office.

So this successful exercise I just described, and it is a conscious exercise, I practice all day, every day of my life with myself, my mind, my internal team, my clients, my vendors, my contractors, with the kid that serves me my Starbucks coffee daily, with the guy that cuts me offonthefreeway,withjustabouteveryonethatIinteractwith.That understanding is really the secret that has worked out for me in my daily practice of life and leadership. Some of the folks in my office that know me well, are already very good at it, and while they may chuckle and love to tease me, they know it works. I must say I am proud when I see the beginning of their employment of these tactics.

The fact is we are nothing but energy, and we all belong to a world that is so abundant it is mind blowing, when we are at peace with ourselves, our minds, our internal selves, we will lead in an effortless way. When we understand how we operate, and we listen, observe and understand those we are working and living with, and we shift the energy pattern to understand them, while maintaining our own boundaries, is the moment we are leading. When we use that understanding as a tool to access what we want is the moment we are not only succeeding but leading.

When we learn to live life with joy, to truly enjoy the daily work and interaction with others that life gives us, is when we are abundant and we have succeeded and life is but a dream.

Today in my office we are enjoying, gratefully so, one of the biggest booms in my company. We have opened an office in downtown Beverly Hills and we are enjoying an abundance of projects and sales orders unprecedented. I personally am grateful just about every moment that I possibly can and I am thoroughly enjoying my daily life, the work we are doing, as well as the products we are producing. Challenges, conflicts and troubles do arise of course, but I now see them as blessings to allow my team and I to see how resourceful and how strong we are. We have seen wonderful things happen that would have been unimaginable a few years ago. The journey has been a true delight for me and for that I am grateful always. As I am grateful to my team for the amazing lessons they teach me on a daily basis.

---

1   Please note that Spirit is an interchangeable term. The importance is in discovering something greater than yourself, which can be identified by a variety of names or ideas, whatever works for you. Referring to it as the "Spirit" has been what works best for me in my spiritual practice. I encourage you to use whatever term, belief or name creates a sense of faith for you.

BIOGRAPHY

Rey III Viquez employs elegant design as a powerful tool to catapult you into an experience that will captivate and jolt all your senses and your behavioral precedents. A true artist that believes his dedication to spiritual practice of daily meditation and connection to his internal source of energy is at the core of his business success.

Founder of *The Rey3 Design* based in Beverly Hills does everything from luxury residential and commercial projects to innovative superyacht interior designs.

CHAPTER SIX

JOEL LOPEZ GARCIA

7 TRAITS EVERY LEADER MUST HAVE

We're living in a time when most of us have a skewed idea of success. We're constantly looking at other people and comparing ourselves to them. Social media makes this habit a constant. But for anyone who is a leader or striving to be one, this misplaced attention and wasted energy should be avoided.

Leaders should not buy into the fallacy of thinking that just because the media tells you "This is what success looks like," that's the only way. Don't compare yourself with the people you think are successful — you don't know their situation. You don't know where they came from. You don't know what kind of help they had. Most importantly, you don't know about all the challenges those people had to overcome to achieve that level of success. Keep in mind, there is a big difference between comparing yourself to other people and looking up to people or having mentors – the former will hinder you in your journey and the latter will help you attain your goals.

Everybody should have their own definition of success. For some people, it's monetary. It's financial. For some people, it's more about the freedom aspect of being able to do whatever they want to do, whenever. Those are the people who create — they're meant to be leaders. Those are the ones with the drive to lead others, to do great things and build and fix things. They are the kind of people who are open to possibilities and see solutions where others see problems.

I fall into that camp. I believe successful leaders have some innate skills, but most of what makes them successful needs to be self-taught. They also need to hold onto that feeling they had when they were young, when the whole world was open to them and everything seemed conceivable. As a successful real estate entrepreneur, I fear losing that feeling I would have as a kid when everything seemed possible. I need to constantly be challenged, but lately I've become comfortable in the niche of flipping houses of a median price range. Flipping houses is my specialty, but I may need to change things up a bit if I want to continue growing. Fear stops me from moving forward, but I'll overcome it. I always do. It's always a good idea to welcome challenges because it's the only way to learn and improve yourself.

Consider when you were a kid and anything and everything seemed possible. Maybe you wanted to be president. When I was growing up, I really and truly believed I was going to move to New York City one day and play ball for the Yankees. I was convinced that was what I was going to do, and I believed it. I don't know why people lose that sense when they grow up.

I wanted to be everything. Around the age of 4-5, I would come out in the morning and pretend to sell my family sopes, which are a traditional Mexican dish — sort of like tacos but better. At one moment, I'd want to be a cook making and selling delicious food and the next I'd want to be a firefighter or an architect.

In many ways, after years of developing myself and building several businesses, I am living out a dream. It may not be exactly one of the ones I had as a child, but it makes good on the feeling I had that I would always be a leader. I hope my story will inspire others to get back that childhood sense of "anything is possible" and make good on their dreams of becoming a successful leader or improving the one they are today.

I may still be young but I've learned some valuable lessons that can take some people decades to realize. I've put those lessons into my work and into my development as a leader today. Just as I see the potential in the worn-down houses that I flip and turn into profitable homes, people along the way saw potential in me, and I'm doing the same for my employees. My parents and the mentors I've been lucky enough to meet have shown me the way.

I work hard now, but when I was young I veered away from the strong work ethic my parents eventually instilled in me from their own experiences. My parents and I migrated to the U.S. from Mexico when I was 10 years old with pretty much nothing but the clothes on our backs. My mother and father had to work longer hours and harder when they came here so that they could provide me with more opportunities and access to a better future.

Like any kid, I wanted to be cool. And I also had my eye on becoming a leader. Unfortunately, the cool kids in the schools I attended, the leaders, were the troublemakers. So that's who I gravitated to, and I became one of them. I got into fights and got kicked out of schools.

The troublemaking cycle I was on died down in the later years of high school. I consider eighth and ninth grades to be my worst years. I got kicked out of school in ninth grade for hanging out with the wrong crowd. The new school wanted me to play baseball, one of my passions. I was thrilled. But soon after, the bones in my finger were shattered into different pieces in an accident, and I could no longer play. I couldn't throw the ball anymore. I could have become consumed by this setback, but instead it gave me purpose. I started to really focus more in my schoolwork. Getting good grades wasn't hard for me. One of my school counselors noticed I had potential and suggested I take some college courses. The classes I took at a community college helped me out a lot. It exposed me to other concepts and kept me engaged.

In fact, years later, I still strongly believe in the value of education. I think we should all make an effort to continue learning. My parents instilled this in me, even when I wasn't on board. They stood up for me and made sure I always got back on the right path.

In spite of all my problems in my early high school years, I graduated with honors and went on to graduate magna cum laude from UCLA and I was accepted to three of the top 10 law schools. Unfortunately, I couldn't afford to continue my education at that time. Not one to sit still, I wanted and needed to start working. As luck would have it, I graduated during one of the worst economies in the country's history. The housing market had crashed and jobs for college graduates were scarce. I soon realized, however, that — at least for me — this economic crisis would not be as big a deal as it was for others.

There was opportunity in the downturn, and I was going after it. I had aspirations and they did not involve having "assistant" in my title.

I took a chance and went into real estate, an industry I had paid attention to since I was young. I had even helped my parents refinance their home while still in high school. In the Latino community, whoever knows the language of the sale best basically turns into the translator of the whole family. So I helped them get that deal done.

Starting out in real estate wasn't easy. I had to learn what to do from the very bottom. One of my current business partners, a fraternity brother, was willing to show me the ropes in the real estate market. "I want to learn," I told him. "Teach me. I'm not expecting you to pay me by the hour or a salary." He connected me with another fraternity brother, who was a real estate broker. I became a transaction coordinator, which at first involved a lot of paper pushing. Loan modifications were a huge thing at the time. Everyone was trying to take advantage of lower interest rates and also redo their mortgages so they could afford to keep their homes. By shadowing both of my fraternity brothers, I was learning the ins and outs of being a real estate agent and a lender. I did some refinancing and I closed some sales, but I felt unchallenged.

I wanted to do more. I wanted to open my own shop, so to speak. At the height of the financial crisis, between 2008 and 2009, house auctions were becoming more prevalent. I would print out their auction listings and just go and watch them sell the assets of huge banks. It was a surreal experience and it became life changing once I realized how cheap houses were going for. Some were just $50,000.

My excitement might have gotten the better of me. I had just sold my most prized possessions at the time, which were my motorcycle and car. I used that cash and pooled my funds with my family's and a family friend for some working capital. We had lofty goals in those early days of what would later become my business. The whole process took way longer than I expected. We made so many mistakes. We tried to do the work ourselves. Obviously, a contractor can do the work much faster than someone who is not in the construction industry.

My first flip was a flop. It took us almost two years from the date of purchase to the actual resale. In the end, even though we made a sizeable profit, it was not a great deal because of the amount of time it took between the time we made the purchase to when it sold again. However, the whole transaction made me realize that flipping houses is doable, and it gave me hope. After this experience, I felt like I could actually create something on my own. I went back to my school — at least my own version of school. I read up on everything and anything to do with the real estate market, I studied the key players, I attended seminars, I reached out to people, and most importantly I took massive action.

Fast forward a few years and now I have five different streams of income from my real estate business. My main bread and butter is still flipping houses. We buy homes at auctions, and we also buy them directly from homeowners, tax liens, probates, you name it. As long as we're able to get a deal on the property, we bite. We're always looking for new properties. We buy them with cash, so we easily outbid our competitors. And the homeowners are happy to make a connection with us because they get a better deal in the long run — they don't have to pay the high commission that real estate agents charge and they don't have to pay any closing costs. Perhaps even better for them is the fact we don't haggle over the details like some buyers do. We take the property as is, and then we fix them up, and we flip them for a profit.

My business team is made up of real estate agents, lenders, escrow officers, title insurance representatives, assistants, property finders, construction workers, project managers and contractors. How do I guide them to keep us successful? A big part of leadership is innate. It will get better over time, but you need a foundation. I'm not talking about intelligence here — although that's helpful — what matters is persistence and diligence. Some people have certain special qualities that make them a good leader. Really good leaders know how to hone their skills and become successful in their field. They have the following traits:

You have extensive interpersonal skills: Strong leaders know how to read people well, and this skill allows them to connect with people on a more personal level no matter the circumstance. This is an innate skill. You either have it or you don't. When people see you as a leader, you should know that you have a unique gift. This gift should be polished. You can always improve.

You love to learn: Every day I want to become a better version of myself. I crave new experiences and look for opportunities to educate and develop myself. Leaders need to be humble enough to know that they can never stop learning, especially because they have a team that depends on them and the hard decisions that they need to make. Never stop learning and never stop reading. The more you read and the more you learn, the more you realize how little you know or how much you still have to learn. I highly recommend 7 *Habits of Really Successful People; Rich Dad, Poor Dad; Millionaire Next Door; Think and Grow Rich;* and *The One Thing.*

You're willing to go all in: Always be determined and committed to driving excellent results. I'm very diligent with my work, with my numbers, especially when I'm investing other people's money. I have to treat my private investors' money as if it's mine. This means performing due diligence with each and every investment. I do my research and make sure I don't leave any stone unturned. I also invest my own capital alongside my investors' money on most of my deals because I want my investors to feel like, "Hey, you know what? He's truly invested." They know I'm committed, that I'm going all in. One of my biggest fears is finding out that something I did — or didn't do — leads to a negative result. When I've done my homework and when I have skin in the deal, then I'm more likely to see a positive outcome.

You highly value time: Time is an asset you can't get back. You can't buy or produce any more time, so be very discriminatory when dealing with time. I like to call this an immigrant mentality. Know that tomorrow is not promised. Don't ever tell yourself, "Oh, I'm going to get it done tomorrow." No. Get it done today. You don't know if tomorrow's promised. Get as much done as possible. Value your time. This is true in business as well as with family. If you are spending time with family, value your time with them. Tomorrow is not promised to any of us.

You have patience when it comes to success: A leader has to have patience. There's no such thing as an overnight success. There are no overnight rock stars. You have got to be willing and able to put in the time. Put in the time and grind it out. Prepare for some failures but power through it. There's a saying that goes, "You've got to fail forward." I can attest to that; I've had a lot of failures but ultimately, those failures are kind of what made me a better professional, a better leader per se. That has allowed me to have what I consider a satisfying level of success. But I'm still not where I want to ultimately be. So I'm patient at the moment, knowing that I'm just scratching the surface.

You're always creating: When you own your own business, that's a creation. You're creating your business. You're creating your own opportunities. A lot of people in businesses that are struggling, they need to create possibilities. They need to keep creating — I say, "If a thousand doors close on you, there's going to be that one door that's going to open, and if not, build your own door." Don't lose that childhood curiosity and naiveté of being open to create new things without the fear of criticism.

You lead from behind and build horizontal relationships: Get out of the office and get into the trenches. I'm constantly at work sites. I don't think I'm better than my staff and they know it. I work alongside them. I know a lot more about construction because of that, and if a project is about to get stalled, I can jump in and get things done. I have built horizontal relationships with my employees, my investors, and my partners. Some people cut themselves off from the people they work with and have only vertical relationships — they look down at people and operate through a hierarchy. In my business, I make sure to have horizontal relationships with people, so I can connect in a much more personal level. I treat my investors the same way I treat one of my painters or project managers. Tight relationships enable leaders to manage situations whether the people involved are good or bad. A lot of my work involves word of mouth, and I'm very big on social media accessibility, so I encourage people to follow me on social media and engage with me (my handle on Periscope and Instagram is Realestatepreneur™).

What's next for me? I still have the dreaming mentality of when I was a little kid. I'd love my company name to be on a skyscraper some day. I'd love to become one of the biggest developers in the nation, a real estate mogul. To get there, I'm thinking about what future communities will look like. Self-sustaining communities are what's next. The technology is there to make it possible, as solar energy continues to gain ground and more affordable eco-friendly materials become available.

I know I need to be patient. When I talk about my ultimate goals, I know that's not going to happen overnight. I know that's not going to happen next month. I know it's not going to happen next year. It might take five, ten, fifteen years, but ultimately, that's where I want to get to.

In any industry, there are levels. Even when you start your own business, you're taking a leap a faith. You're putting everything on the line and sometimes it works out, sometimes it doesn't. It's kind of the same thing whenever you hit a plateau. Some people stay in the same place because they're comfortable there. A lot of times, you need a jolt, to recall that same feeling you had when you started your business. Tap into the raw energy and pure confidence that got you going and know that you can take a leap again, to go after bigger projects and take on new challenges, and start raising more capital to make it all happen.

Most leaders, once they achieve a certain level of success, they have this feeling inside of wanting to give back. I see it a lot with first-generation entrepreneurs as well as successful entrepreneurs. They have this feeling of wanting to give back and wanting to lend a helping hand for the next generation. Once you achieve that level of success, that interpretation that you have of success, you should help others do that same thing.

It's an exciting time to be in business. I'm really excited about the possibilities that are opening up, particularly when it comes to raising capital. The deregulation of crowdfunding will open up the doors for a lot of entrepreneurs and investors as well. Some people will be able to receive the same type of returns that some of our private investors are receiving with less money out of pocket.

This change in the market will bring positive changes for my business too. That might enable us to go out and start developing. We'd start out small, maybe with smaller lots and smaller communities. I've been in talks with a few people who do this already, and I've been looking at projects. I haven't pulled the trigger on any of them because of fear. Fear is never going to go away. What makes one leader stand out from another is how we handle fear.

There will always be a fear of failure. I hate failing. Who doesn't? But it's reality and an important ingredient of entrepreneurship. People who have created successful businesses and have proven to be strong leaders have all had failures at some point. It's what they do next that matters. Do they give up or do they pick themselves up and become determined to improve? I try to avoid failures, of course, but I've learned to embrace them and learn from them. Learning from our mistakes is how we develop ourselves, better ourselves. It's how we become better leaders, and in my case, a better investor.

It is said that what we should really fear is not failure but rather turning into a person who is no longer brave enough to take risks and embrace challenges. That's a person who has given up. I've come far but I know I have room to grow. And I'm going after whatever is next. In some ways, I'm just getting started.

BIOGRAPHY

Joel Lopez Garcia is the CEO & Founder of LG Capital Group and Managing partner of companies ranging from Real Estate to the auto-leasing ride sharing industry. His passion for Real Estate is only rivaled by his passion for personal development and Boba drinks(Seriously!). Above all, he lives for his family and he is passionate about making something out of nothing, making a way out of no way and beautifying communities by turning properties from neighborhood eyesores to beautiful homes for families – all while making great returns for his companies and private investors. Joel Lopez Garcia is the @RealEstatepreneur; he is also a son, grandson, husband, Nu Alpha Kappa Inc. Fraternity brother, millennial and dog parent.

CHAPTER SEVEN
MARCOS OROZCO

During my teenage years when I was anointed, along with 9 others, to be the representative of a group of over 1,000 delinquent teenagers. Long before that I was born in Nicaragua during a dangerous revolution. We had to flee. We didn't tell anyone that we were leaving because it was too dangerous. Luckily for our family, we had visas that my aunt and uncle in the United States helped us receive. Everything happened so quickly and so quietly. We didn't even sell our house or anything inside of it. We just fled the revolution with the clothes on our back and what ever we could fit in our luggage.

We flew to the United States and ended up living in Redondo Beach California. Living in the beach area was an amazing experience for me as a youth. I got to spend a couple of summers eating peanut butter and jelly sandwiches on the sand. The elementary school I went to at that time was mostly made up of white kids with a sprinkle of other ethnic groups. I was one of only seven Latinos.

Since I didn't know how to speak English, some kids would make fun of me. But that only encouraged me to learn the language quickly. We were there for a couple of years until my father decided to move our family to Gardena, California. Gardena is located between South Central and Compton. Two cities filled with drugs and gangs. My father didn't know any better, but crack cocaine was just being introduced to the streets of Los Angeles. This made the streets feel like a war zone. Ironically, my parents left Nicaragua because they wanted to move to a safer place.

As soon as we moved to Gardena I noticed that everything was different. Especially in elementary school. I saw the difference in cultures. From being in the Beach City to the Inner city was a huge change. I saw kids break dancing. I started noticing graffiti in the bathrooms and in the streets which sparked my curiosity. I heard rap music and that intrigued me. I even started break dancing with my friends and neighbors in the alley near my house. I started writing on walls at that young age and started adapting to my environment. Then there were shifts from one counterculture to another. From break dancing to BMX riding to skateboarding. Skateboarding with the local kids and my cousins was the best time of my life. We would gather at my cousin Eric's house and watch Powel Peralta's skating videos and try to mimic them for hours. Unbeknownst to me, this was developing my strong work ethic that I feel so grateful for today.

Another transition of trends was from skateboarding to joining the local gang. You could be independent, but this was probably going to earn you a couple of fist fights. During this time I became fascinated with graffiti and started writing on walls. I was so naïve that I didn't even know it was against the law. I started becoming what they call a "graffiti artist" and started connecting with other of the local

94

artists. I painted murals, wrote on walls, and on RTD buses. The graffiti movement in Los Angeles exploded and eventually, the older kids of the neighborhood graffiti crew recruited me.

One time, we were having issues with another group from another city. There had been some fights and confrontations. That's when my friends Case and Zeres (rest in peace), among others, decided it was better to join forces. Everything changed after that.

Separate, nobody knew who we were. We had had very little impact. But together, we became the most respected graffiti art crew in all of the South Bay and Orange County. We started building respect, which led to new enemies in Los Angeles in the '90s.

Since I was one of the originals from the group, I was anointed as the leader of the Gardena Chapter along with my friend, Eddie Casillas (Rest in piece). We were in charge of Leading around 100 other teenagers in our click in Gardena know as "The 4 clique". Our crew was over 1,000 strong, so there were about 10 to 12 leaders in our organization. This is where my leadership skills started to come to fruition. Even though I didn't have a formal leadership education, I knew that people listened to me because I was a firm believer in what I did and I did what I said. I was also filled with confidence and always considered myself a defender of the damned. I would stand up to kids that were targets of bullies. So it made it easier for others to trust and confide in me.

During this time the streets of Los Angeles were very dangerous. NWA came out with their 1st album and it felt like that was the match that set off a bomb in the streets. The streets were flooded with cheap crack cocaine and the local gangs were fighting for drug turf with semi-automatic rifles and Uzis. This was the recipe for the perfect storm of violence and blood shed. This was becoming the norm in Los Angeles. It was becoming part of its culture. It was being packaged and sold as music videos to the inner city youth and they loved it. We loved it.

We started mimicking the rappers and drug dealers. These were the role models we grew up with. We did everything we saw in the music videos. We drank 40 oz. beer cans and bottles, sold and smoked weed. We wanted to drive big Cadillacs and 64 Impalas with hydraulics. We dressed and talked like them and we adopted the violent lifestyle as well. We thought it was cool until things got real, real quick.

My friends started dying from gun violence and drug overdoses. I started attending so many of my friends' funerals that I started planning my own at the age of 17. I remember attending my friend and co-leader Eddie Casillas' funeral and thinking to myself, "When I die, I'm going to have the biggest funeral, way bigger than this one!" I was actually pretty excited about it. It was going to be like a big party! I had a location, a song, and a guest list. I wanted to be buried in Roosevelt Memorial Park on Vermont right across the street from Ascot Raceway Park in Gardena so that my friends could visit me often, smoke weed, and drink beer at my tombstone.

During my friend Bernie's funeral, they played a song from La Bamba. Afterwards, every time I heard that song, I thought of him. Wanting to be remembered as well, I picked out my own song. "I'll Take You There" by the Staple Singers which is still one of my favorite songs.

Since I was a popular kid, I had a giant list of names and the phone numbers of my friends I wanted to attend my funeral. I carried that list in my wallet in a folded piece of paper so that my mother could call and invite them to my last shindig after I died. It just felt like the natural thing to do and to be honest, I couldn't have been the only teenager who didn't think he was not going to make it to his 21st birthday. Years later I realized that it was my foundation of strong values and morals that my parents gifted me along with my leadership skills that kept my alive.

Now lets fast-forward. After I cleaned up and wanted to be successful, I developed companies and employed many people. I had to develop leadership skills the more traditional way, with books, experience, and education. Before we dive in to the characteristics of great leaders, I want to talk about 3 myths about leadership.

Myth Number 1: The myth of "Natural born leaders" That great leaders are born that way. That is not true at all. There are people that are born with leadership traits that grow up to be better leaders when they nurture and cultivate their gift, but nobody is just born a great leader. Napoleon didn't just come out of his mother's womb and started leading France. He worked hard.

You have to develop that gift just like any athlete would develop and hone their talent.

Myth Number 2: The alpha male leader myth. Hollywood has painted this for us very well. An example is that movie scene where John Wayne kicks the door open, pounds his chest and starts telling everyone what to do and then they follow him.

That's not how it really works. That's a romanticized view of leadership created by Hollywood. That's a big misconception about leadership. As a matter of fact, that's not very effective in today's world.

Myth Number 3: Leaders are great managers. Absolutely false. Managers and leadership have very different skillsets. Some leaders are not great managers and vice versa. I'm a big believer on focusing on what you are good at. Good managers manage people, processes, and protocols. Leaders have a different role. They lead managers, they sell the vision, and they see the bigger picture. Needles to say, great managers often become excellent leaders.

Now let's talk about some of the important traits leaders have from my own experience.

Great leaders are humble. They come from a place of service. They don't consider themselves better than anyone else. We've all known an arrogant person in a leadership role. There's not much loyalty behind someone like that. The ego often limits and destroys organizations.

Leaders are confident. Keep in mind that confidence and arrogance are very distinct. Confidence comes from experience and understanding. I have a company called BookFamous.com and I have helped many people write and self publish their first book so that they can stand out in their industry, leverage their message, and generate more income. Even if they don't have the time. We have launched so many best sellers that my company and I are confident in our process. This can only happen because we have "walked though the dessert" ourselves and now, with confidence, help others walk through the dessert as well.

Having an abundant mindset is one of the most important attributes of a great leader. They are not afraid to create other leaders. They know that there is enough success for anyone who wants to pursue it. They exude this great energy of abundance and love to give.

Leaders also care about people. They care about their tribe. Great leaders genuinely like people. They tend to relate to the people they lead. They often see themselves as an equal. They try to make this world a better place for every one of their tribe members.

Leaders do not abuse their power, they respect it. Power drunk leaders often become tyrants. History has a great record of the outcome of these tyrants and it's never good for the people or themselves. Napoleon let it go to his head, for example. Voltaire is famous for saying, "With great power comes great responsibility."

Great leaders are cheerleaders. They love to cheer people on. They love to applaud and make others feel better about themselves. They love to nurture their tribe with positive feedback. Don't mistake this kindness for weakness. Leaders are also stern when need be. There is a fine balance of boundaries and kindness that is often learned through years of practice and trials and errors.

Great leaders also take full responsibility for when things go bad. This is very difficult to practice, but very important. When something goes bad, a great leader steps in and takes full responsibility for whatever happened. They also give credit when good things happen to the team. They don't jump in on the spotlight. They actually enjoy giving credit and praise the team that helped them.

Leaders are students. They're into self-development. They're always honing in on their skills. Leaders are also great listeners. They listen to the tribe members for feedback.

Leaders are problem solvers. They don't panic at obstacles, they asses the situation and focus on the outcome. They don't need to be right, they focus on solutions.

Leaders are visionaries. They see the big picture and are usually years ahead of their time. It takes a lot of courage to lead others because they at times make tough decisions and these decisions oftentimes affect the livelihood of others.

Leaders know when to pivot. This is very important in business as well. Businesses pivot when their initial plan isn't working so they have to try a new one. They mustn't be afraid to change. Similarly, leaders admit when they're wrong or when something isn't working. No one is perfect and to become more influential with your people, sometimes you have to come clean about previous mistakes.

These are the important characteristics and habits of great leaders.

Now that you know what it takes, I'm going to give you 3 simple things that you can do to become a better leader, today.

Number one: The most important thing you have to do is decide if you want to become a leader. I know it sounds simple or a no brainer, but it's not. A lot of people struggle with this. If you don't want to be a great leader, there is no reason to even try. Believe it or not, everybody is a leader. Everybody has to lead themselves. But not everybody is a great leader. I believe there are more ineffective leaders than we would like to admit. If being a great leader is important to you, that's the first step. Decide and declare it to yourself.

Number two: Improve your communication skills. One of the best ways to do this is to monitor yourself.

If you talk on the phone with somebody, record that phone conversation. Take note of how you communicate. What words do you use? Are you calm? Do you let the other person speak? You'll learn a lot from hearing yourself speak. Learn some basic communication skills and build from there. It's very important to be able to communicate how you think, what you feel, and what you want, to those that you are leading.

Number three: Get a mentor. All leaders have mentors that help them grow and get them out of their comfort zone. We often learn so much more and so much quicker from mentors because they have already been there. They have been in these situations before. It's like reading a book. You get someone's lifetime of lessons without having to live it yourself. If you have a question or a problem, chances are someone has had that problem before and someone has solved it before.

In closing, leadership issues tend to bleed into other areas of your life. If your business is failing, if you're having issues with your family, if your bank account is a little bit on the needy side, these are all symptoms of leadership issues. I have consulted dozens of companies in the past and 99% of the time, there are problems with leadership. Once you identify what the problems are, you have to take full accountability for them and take action towards fixing them. But it truly begins with you. Leadership is one of the most important skills you will ever learn and one that will pay off the most. Not just financially, but in life and legacy. I want you to know that I believe in you and will always root for you from the sidelines!

BIOGRAPHY

Marcos Orozco is an Influential Speaker, Best Selling Author, Founder of Gentepreneur.com and BookFamous.com As thought leader for the Latino Success Movement, He is dedicated to helping American Latinos succeed in business. A Nicaraguan immigrant who struggled, survived and thrived in the Drug and Gang infested neighborhood of Gardena, California. He battled addictions, depression and was even planning his own funeral at the age of 17 because many of his friends where being killed in the violent streets. When the dust settled, he went on to Successfully launching multiple ventures for over a decade, claims that the secret to his success is in his failures. Marcos loves to spend quality time with his son.

CONCLUSION

We would like to conclude this book with a simple message of hope and responsibility. This book was written by 7 different authors with different experiences and circumstances. We want you to know that Leadership starts with you and should not be delegated to anyone else. You don't need a fancy title or permission from anyone to be a great leader, but know that you have the power to lead people to do great things at incredible scale if you chose to do so. Leadership begins with you!

CONNECT WITH THE AUTHORS!!

Please register by visiting the website, and get instant access to **videos** that connects you to each author. Simply go to:

www.LeadershipHabitsBook.com